MANX RAILWAYS
& TRAMWAYS

E D W A R D   G R A Y

Sutton Publishing Limited
Phoenix Mill · Thrupp · Stroud
Gloucestershire · GL5 2BU

First published 1998

British Library Cataloguing in Publication Data
A catalogue record for this book is available from the
British Library.

ISBN 0-7509-1827-6

Typeset in 10/12 Perpetua.
Typesetting and origination by
Sutton Publishing Limited.
Printed in Great Britain by
Ebenezer Baylis, Worcester.

Manx Electric Railway cars 1 and 2, dating from 1893, pictured at Laxey in 1997. They are the oldest tramcars in the world still in regular use on their original line. (E. Gray)

CONTENTS

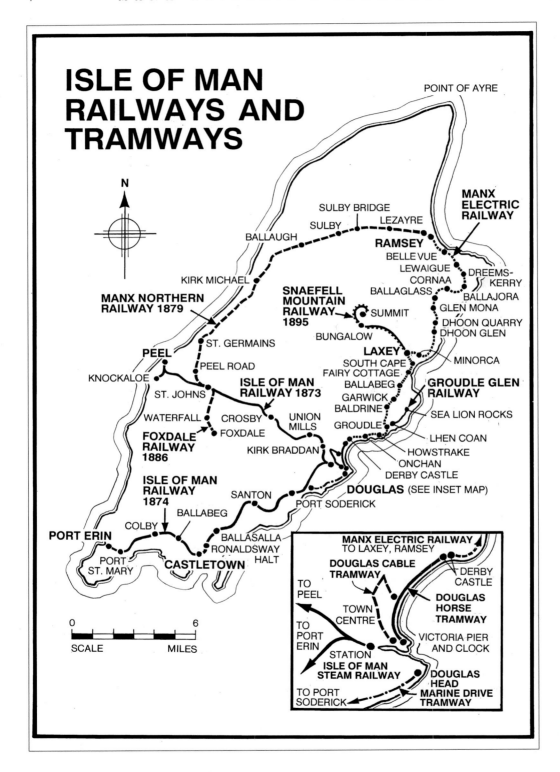

ISLE OF MAN RAILWAYS AND TRAMWAYS

INTRODUCTION

VICTORIA PIER, DOUGLAS, I. O. M.

The Isle of Man, a mere 30 miles long and 12 miles wide, is a hilly island, set in the middle of the Irish Sea. Hitherto a sparsely populated land of herring fishermen, farmers and miners, major changes to the economy occurred in the latter half of the nineteenth century, when the island began to enjoy an unprecedented tourist boom. In summertime, the resident population was swollen by many thousands of visitors, attracted by the island's charming scenery and pleasant climate. Steamers carried thousands of holiday-makers from mainland ports, and the island became, as one railway prospectus described it, 'one of the favourite watering places of the north of England'. The island's land-based transport systems were developed to carry visitors inland or to places of interest around the coast. Within its small area, the Isle of Man pioneered an unusual variety of railway and tramway undertakings, some operating only in the summer season, but others becoming important channels of communication for the island's residents.

The majority of holiday-makers arrived by ship at Douglas. At first, many visitors were deterred from exploring further inland by the island's lack of adequate transport facilities. There were scenic cruises by paddle-steamer to coastal towns such as Port St Mary, Laxey or Ramsey, but boarding-house proprietors and shop-keepers in resorts other than Douglas were anxious to gain a share of the tourist trade, and urged better means of access to the smaller towns.

There had been several abortive schemes to link the ports of Douglas, Castletown, Port Erin, Peel and Ramsey by railway, any of which, had they come to fruition, would have been welcomed by the Manx farmers and miners, who were anxious to transport their produce and livestock more easily. It was not until the Isle of Man Railway Company completed its line across the centre of the island in 1873 that matters began to develop more rapidly. A railway to the south, and another to Ramsey in the north, followed fairly quickly, soon augmented by a branch in the centre of the island designed to transport the rich ores from the Foxdale mines. For the first time, the Isle of Man had a distribution system for its imports and exports. In Douglas, horse and cable tramcars allowed the growing town to expand further, and the north-east corner of the island was opened up by the electric tramway. The Snaefell Mountain Railway, the Douglas Southern Electric tramway, and the Groudle Glen miniature railway were all projects of the 1890s which catered unashamedly for seasonal visitors, exploiting the tourist trade and developing new areas, and all of them increased the prosperity of the island people.

Thus, in a period of only twenty-five years, the Isle of Man gained a rich inheritance of transport treasures, which served the island well for over half a century. Unhappily, drastic changes occurred in the tourist trade after 1950. The easy availability of cheap package holidays to the Continent forced the island to rely less on seasonal visitors. In addition, the spread of car ownership meant that local residents used public transport less. Government concentration on other priorities led some people to believe that the antiquated railways and tramways were merely a burden on the economy, and would be better abandoned. Consequently, the unique transport systems suffered from falling revenue and lack of investment in the 1960s and '70s. Portions of the railway closed, but campaigners fought to save what remained, and a change of heart on the part of the government has ensured that much has survived The Manx tramways and railways are not to be classed with the usual run of preserved museum lines, for they continue to provide useful services in their original settings. Retaining their Victorian charm and using original rolling stock, the lines are now rightly valued as incomparable tourist attractions and receive strong political support. Not profitable in themselves, the railways receive a government subsidy, but in return they generate many millions of pounds for the island's economy.

Today, the Isle of Man offers an amazing transport experience. In summer, horse-drawn tramcars trundle along Douglas promenade, and vintage steam trains work between Douglas and Port Erin. The Manx Electric Railway offers year-round services between Douglas and Ramsey, using some of the oldest electric tramcars in the world on a beautiful scenic line. The first section of the electric tramway celebrated a hundred years of operation in 1993, and the Snaefell Mountain Railway and the Groudle Glen Railway reached their centenaries in 1995. Celebrations are planned for the 125th anniversary of the steam railway, for which locomotive no. 1, *Sutherland*, which opened the line between Douglas and Peel in 1873, is being prepared for a return to service. The centenary of the tramway extension from Laxey to Ramsey is also to be marked by special events. Transport enthusiasts from all over the world are expected to visit the island to participate in the celebrations in 1998. As a steam train has worked successfully on the electric tramway, 1998 plans incorporate the possibility that an electric tramcar will run on the steam railway – now that will be a novelty!

THE ISLE OF MAN RAILWAY

The Isle of Man Railway Company (IMR) opened an 11½-mile 3 ft gauge line from Douglas to Peel on 1 July 1873. A 15½-mile line to the south, linking Douglas with Castletown and Port Erin, was ready by 1 August 1874. There was less enthusiasm for a line to Ramsey because of doubts about its profitability, but the project was taken up by a separate company, the Manx Northern Railway (MNR), and services on a 16½-mile west coast route from St John's via Kirk Michael began on 23 September 1879.

MNR interests formed a nominally independent company, the Foxdale Railway (FR), to build a 2¼-mile branch from St John's to the Foxdale mines in order to transport ore for export via Ramsey. Ready in August 1886, this line joined the MNR track at St John's. Competition from the east coast tramway to Ramsey after 1899, coupled with falling output from the mines, led the MNR into financial difficulties, and in 1905 it was taken over by the IMR. An addition to the system was made in 1915, when a 1-mile branch was constructed from Glenfaba, near Peel, to carry supplies to the alien detention camp at Knockaloe. This was closed in 1920.

Falling revenue and increasing costs led to the complete closure of the railway at the end of the 1965 season. In 1967 the railway revived temporarily when it was leased by the Marquis of Ailsa, but passenger services on the Peel and Ramsey lines ended in 1968. Efforts were then concentrated on the preservation of the South Line. Operation reverted to the Company in 1972. An experimental working in 1975, operating only a curtailed section of line from Castletown, proved disastrous, and a campaign to re-open the full length of the South Line succeeded in 1977. Subsequently the railway was nationalised by the Isle of Man government. Illustrated here is Douglas station in about 1908. It has raised platforms, but as yet lacks canopies. Locomotives 7 Tynwald *and 9* Douglas *stand by the water column ready to assume their turns of duty. (L&GP/NRM)*

Douglas station, looking towards the buffer stops from the signal-box. The North Line platform is to the left, the South Line platform in the centre, and the goods yard on the extreme right. Arriving trains were routed to the inner faces of the two platforms, between which lay the engine-release track. (E. Gray)

Trains normally left Douglas from the outer faces of the platforms. The train leaving from the North Line platform is headed by locomotive no. 8, *Fenella*. The North Line arrival platform is to the right. Platform canopies were constructed in 1909.

In 1873 operation of the Peel line began with three 2–4–0 tank locomotives supplied by Beyer Peacock of Manchester. *Sutherland*, *Derby* and *Pender* were named respectively after the Duke of Sutherland (Company Chairman), Lord Derby and John Pender (Deputy Chairman). The sloping smokebox door, the brass numerals on the chimney, and the bell-mouthed brass dome were typical features. (Real Photographs)

No. 1, *Sutherland*, at Ramsey, 1952. Several alterations were made to the locomotives over the years, some as a result of re-boilering. The original 320-gallon side tanks were replaced by others of larger capacity. Canvas cab-side curtains ('dodgers') were used to shield crews in bad weather. A re-railing jack is mounted on the tank top. (Dr R.P. Hendry)

Crosby station, looking towards Douglas. The railway was single-track, with passing loops at the stations. Intermediate station buildings on the Peel line were small, timber constructions. The white gates are closed to road traffic as the train approaches. To the right is the crossing-keeper's stone lodge. After 1922 all engines ran chimney-first from Douglas; previously the out-stationed locomotives were turned to work chimney-first from their home shed.

The IMR station building at St John's was on the south platform, and was a larger version of the 1873 style at Crosby. Locomotive no. 6, *Peveril*, heads a three-coach train for Peel in the 1930s. Platforms at intermediate stations tended to be low, as here, or non-existent, as at Crosby. The Nestlé's chocolate machine was once a standard feature of railway stations. (L&GP/NRM)

Peel station in the early 1900s, before the provision of platforms. The splendid terminal buildings erected in 1908 later blocked this uninterrupted view of the Oddfellows Arms. The locomotive stands at the head of a train of four-wheeled coaches, ready to depart for Douglas. The harbour is to the left.

This commercial postcard view of Peel shows the location of the station (centre right) alongside the river. The station buildings now include the large structure across the ends of the tracks, as well as a new goods shed. In the foreground, at the extreme right, is the water tower and loco shed.

The South Line reached Port Erin in 1874. The present station is a substantial building erected in 1904 to replace a former wooden structure on the same site. It incorporates waiting and refreshment rooms. The engine shed and goods shed are to the left. Out of the picture to the right were the bay platforms, an area subsequently lost when it was converted to a bus park.

Engine no. 4, *Loch* (Henry Brougham Loch was the island's Governor from 1863 to 1882), is one of two additional locomotives (the other is no. 5, *Mona*) purchased from Beyer Peacock in 1874 for the opening of the South Line. Though similar to the earlier deliveries, the two newcomers had larger tanks and bunkers (and, eventually, larger diameter boilers) to cope with the more severe gradients. Here, *Loch* stands by the water tank and loco shed at Port Erin in 1985. (E. Gray)

Increased traffic soon led to an additional order for a locomotive identical to nos 4 and 5. No. 6, *Peveril*, was delivered in 1875 and was substantially rebuilt to receive larger tanks and boiler in 1911. Pictured here at Peel in 1947, the locomotive was in Tuscan Red livery. Note the patching on the tanks. (L&GP/NRM)

Five years passed before growing traffic led to the order and delivery of another locomotive. No. 7, *Tynwald* arrived in 1880, and was again almost identical to nos 4 and 5. Minor differences included the removal of the nameplate to the forward end of the side tanks and the repositioning of the maker's plate. (L&GP/NRM)

In 1879 the Manx Northern Railway Company sought tenders from the Manchester firms of Beyer Peacock and Sharp Stewart to build two locomotives for their line to Ramsey. Sharp Stewart gained the order, delivery to be made by the end of May. In fact, because of the late delivery of rolling stock, the MNR was worked temporarily by the IMR. Compared to the Beyer Peacock design, the Sharp Stewart engines (later named *Ramsey* and *Northern*) had a more standard appearance.

Two locomotives were insufficient for the MNR, so tenders were sought for a third, to be delivered within three months. Sharp's late delivery of the first order had not impressed, and the contract was awarded to Beyer Peacock. MNR 3 *Thornhill* of 1880 (named after the Chairman's residence, and identical with IMR no. 7, constructed at the same time) is seen here at Kirk Michael, working chimney-first out of Ramsey. (Manx National Heritage)

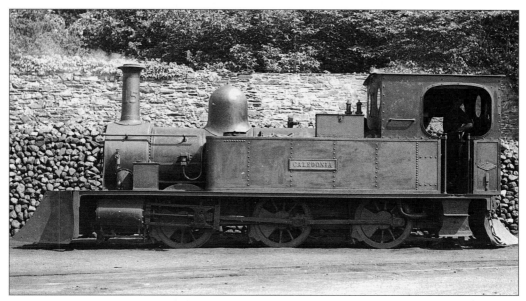

The MNR's fourth (and final) engine, *Caledonia*, was a powerful 0–6–0 tank purchased in 1885 from Dubs of Glasgow. It was considered more suitable than the existing locomotives to haul mineral trains on the steeply graded Foxdale branch. (Coal was hauled from Ramsey to fuel the mine pumping engines, and ore from the Foxdale mines was exported via Ramsey.) *Caledonia*'s longer wheelbase made it unsuitable for sharp curves and later (as IMR 15) it was little used except for snow-clearing duties. (RAS Marketing)

MNR no. 3, *Thornhill*, being similar to the existing IMR engines, was gladly received into the locomotive stud when the MNR was taken over in 1905. New numbers for the ex-MNR engines were not allocated until 1910, and not displayed until much later. *Thornhill* became IMR 14 and is seen here, appropriately, at her home base in Ramsey. The Sharp Stewart locomotives were to be IMR 16 and 17, but never carried these numbers and were withdrawn early. (Roy Brook)

The MNR line from Ramsey (left) met and ran alongside the IMR line from Peel (right) west of St John's. The Foxdale line junction faced towards Ramsey, and led off the MNR track just beyond the second signal, which controlled entry to the branch. The Peel and Ramsey tracks were not connected except at the far end of the IMR St John's station layout. Passengers between Ramsey and Douglas had to change trains until 1881, when a through coach was introduced.

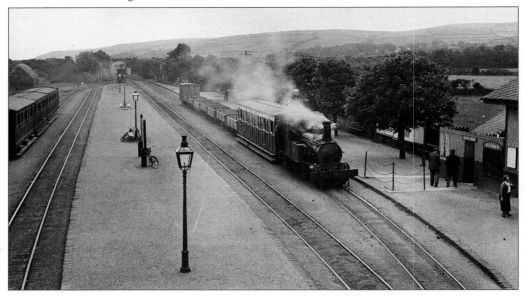

St John's IMR station, looking east, with a train at the Peel platform. MNR trains terminated on a separate site (behind the photographer; see lower picture on page 28) and the Foxdale branch had its own station, from which the line climbed to cross the IMR by the overbridge in the distance. In 1886 St John's thus had three adjacent stations. After the IMR take-over of the MNR, Ramsey trains used the IMR station. From 1927 Foxdale passenger trains also used this station, by joining the Ramsey line and reversing. (L&G/NRM)

The Foxdale branch had a gradient of 1 in 48 and ended in a terminal loading bay by a small station set amid the spoil heaps. Behind the building a line crossed the road to enter the mine premises. The track lay-out included a 'scissors' crossover (centre right) beyond the water tank. In later years, the station became a home for the guard of the Foxdale train.

Output from the Foxdale mines fell and passenger traffic was so light that a single coach sufficed. Mining ceased altogether in 1911, and from mid-1912 the station was closed except during the arrival and departure times of each train. Here, no. 8, *Fenella*, receives attention from the driver while waiting to leave with the Foxdale coach for St John's, a roster usually fitted in by the locomotive crew between other duties. (L&G/NRM)

Locomotive no. 8, *Fenella*, was delivered in 1894, the only new engine of that year. Built by Beyer Peacock to the near-original design, it received several modifications over the years, but retained its original small 385-gallon capacity tanks. The locomotive has a full head of steam as it prepares for duty outside the Douglas sheds in about 1965. (Manx Press Pictures)

Locomotive no. 9, *Douglas*, seen here at St John's, was delivered in 1896, the last of the small-boilered engines. Subsequent orders, eleven years later, were for larger engines. Having suffered no major alterations, except for the provision of sanding gear and vacuum fittings, *Douglas* is the only example of the first series of IMR locomotives to remain in original condition. (Dr R.P. Hendry)

The IMR's take-over of the MNR created a need for larger-boilered engines to work the 26-mile journey from Douglas to Ramsey. In addition there was heavier traffic on the South Line. Beyer Peacock obliged once again, and no. 10, *G.H. Wood* (named after George Henry Wood, first Secretary of the Company), entered service in 1905. Pictured at Douglas in 1965, the engine had lost its taller graceful chimney and numerals. (Manx Press Pictures)

No. 11, *Maitland* (named after Dalrymple Maitland, a Company board member), was the second of the larger engines to arrive in 1905. The two new arrivals were ordered partly to replace the unpopular ex-MNR Sharp Stewart engines and partly because their larger boilers and tanks and longer wheelbases made them more suitable for the heavy South Line traffic. *Maitland* is seen here at Port Erin in 1985. (E. Gray)

Another Beyer Peacock order for a similar locomotive saw the delivery of no. 12, *Hutchinson*, in 1908. Named after William A. Hutchinson, a Company board member, it was similar to nos 10 and 11, and had an extended wheelbase and 480-gallon capacity tanks. It was claimed that the larger engines were better able to run to time. It is seen here at Douglas station in 1938. (G. Harrop)

Douglas station, 1963. Locomotive no. 13 *Kissack* (left), stands at the head of a train on the North Line platform, while no. 16, *Mannin*, waits on the engine-release road. *Kissack*, named after Edward Thomas Kissack, a Company board member, was delivered in 1910, the last of the 10–13 series. *Mannin*, of 1926, was the last new steam engine purchased by the railway. The coupling devices projecting from the centre of the buffer beams were used in conjunction with side chains. (Manx Press Pictures)

Between 1909 and 1926, twenty-six bogie carriages, numbered in series from F50 to F75 and known as 'The Pairs', were created by mounting pairs of former four-wheel bodies on bogie underframes. At first, a space was left between the body ends. The gaps were covered over in the 1930s, but remained distinguishable, as seen here on coach F54 in Douglas station. (E. Gray)

In the goods yard beyond the passenger platforms at Douglas could be seen evidence of the once-lively commercial traffic. At one time, the Company owned some 175 items of goods rolling stock, made up of a mixture of open and roofed wagons, cattle trucks, and miscellaneous vehicles. The carriage of livestock was especially important on market days.

Trains approaching Douglas station were controlled by semaphore signals mounted on a large gantry by the workshop wall. Signals on the left-hand post applied to trains from the Peel line, those on the right to trains on the South Line, the higher arms indicating the arrival platforms. A cross-over just beyond the gantry was the only link (apart from the engine-release roads) between the North and South Lines. To the right are the headshunt tracks leading to the goods yard (centre) and the carriage shed (right). (E. Gray)

Heavy trains leaving Douglas sometimes received help from a banking engine. South Line trains in particular often needed assistance in tackling the adverse gradient at the start of the climb through the Nunnery cutting. Here, no. 8, *Fenella*, banks a Port Erin train as it passes the workshops (right) and the signal-box. The only other signal-box on the island was at St John's.

Engines usually arrived at Douglas bunker first. Stopping clear of the points at the end of the arrival platforms, the locomotive would uncouple from its carriages and move forward to the buffer stops before reversing to run round the train via the centre release road. Here, no. 1 *Sutherland* stands at the head of the arrival track. (E. Gray)

A serious accident occurred on 22 August 1925 when a train hauled by locomotive no. 3, *Pender*, having stopped at Union Mills to detach a cattle van, started off again without the brakesmen on board. The train entered Douglas without sufficient brake power and overran the buffer stops, crashing into the concourse area. This accident, in which the driver was killed, led to the fitting of vacuum brakes.

North Line departures were often double-headed out of Douglas, as the train would be divided at St John's. One engine would proceed with the front portion for Peel, the other would take the rear coaches for Ramsey. Here, locomotives 8, *Fenella*, and 5, *Mona*, head the train, while no. 13, *Kissack*, simmers outside the shed. Spare carriage wheels are stored on an isolated length of track. The oval board on the buffer beam was an indication to gatekeepers that a special train was to follow. (Manx Press Pictures)

The first stopping place along the Peel line was the halt at Braddan, where there was a small booking hut. It was busy only on the occasions of open-air Sunday services, when thousands of people would travel out from Douglas on special trains. Here, no. 14, *Thornhill*, waits for returning worshippers in 1933. More carriages and locomotives stand further along the line. (RAS Marketing)

After Braddan came Union Mills, a delightful station with a platform set on a reverse curve, and then Crosby, a small sleepy halt. The gates are closed to road traffic as engine no. 12, *Hutchinson*, passes the crossing-keeper's stone hut as it arrives at Crosby with a train from Douglas in 1956. (RAS Marketing)

For such a quiet location, Crosby had an unusually long passing loop, together with a cattle dock and goods shed. No passengers are visible in this 1964 view as no. 8, *Fenella*, pauses with a two-coach train on the Peel line. The carriage immediately behind the engine is one of the saloon coaches supplied in 1905, distinguishable by the absence of footboards. (RAS Marketing)

The approach to St John's, looking west towards Peel, seen from the Foxdale line overbridge, 1947. The carriage shed is to the right, and ahead the line divides to serve the Peel and Ramsey platforms, whose tracks were connected only at the eastern end of the station layout. With the opening of the Manx Northern Railway, and later the Foxdale branch, St John's became an important junction. (L&G/NRM)

St John's, looking east towards Douglas and the Foxdale line overbridge. St John's boasted the only other signal cabin outside Douglas. It often appeared tranquil, apparently deserted, but periods of intense activity would occur with the simultaneous arrival of trains from Douglas, Peel and Ramsey. Shunting movements to divide trains, add carriages, or take on water would precede the departures, after which silence would descend once again. (Peter Barlow/Adrian Vaughan collection)

A Douglas–Peel train headed by no. 8, *Fenella*, stands at the south platform of St John's in 1965. The Ramsey portion has been detached from the rear, to be taken onward by a locomotive that has just arrived with a train from the North Line. On this occasion, the latter's carriages from Ramsey were coupled to the rear of a Peel–Douglas train. (E. Gray)

Train movements at St John's were controlled either from the signal cabin, or by hand and flag signals. Sometimes a pilot engine from Douglas would return with the train from the North Line, but on this occasion in 1965, traffic being light, passengers from Ramsey were required to change to the newly arrived train from Peel, hauled by no. 5, *Mona*. (E. Gray)

Trains arriving at Peel crossed Mill Road to enter the station precincts, where passengers were greeted by the unmistakable aroma from the kipper factory. The water tower (left) hides a small engine shed, sited immediately behind. Here, no. 12, *Hutchinson*, stands ready to take on water at Peel in 1954. (Peter Barlow/Adrian Vaughan collection)

West of St John's what appeared to be double track was, in fact, two independent lines. That on the left led to Peel, while that on the right was the Ramsey line, soon veering off northwards. Simultaneous departures saw trains running side-by-side on this stretch. Behind the trees to the right lay the site of the original MNR 1879 terminus and the station building for the Foxdale line. Here, no. 8 *Fenella* arrives with a two-coach train from Ramsey in 1965. (E. Gray)

A few minutes after the previous picture was taken, *Fenella*, having taken on water and run round her train, prepares to depart from St John's with the return working to Ramsey. The MNR line was extended from its original terminus and connected to the IMR at this point in 1881, when through coach working began. From 1904 all trains used the extended trackwork of the IMR station. (E. Gray)

About half a mile west of St John's the North Line began its long climb to the high ground beyond St Germain's where it hugged the cliff tops through a series of cuttings on the way to Kirk Michael. Here, a seven-coach train hauled by *Fenella*, for many years the Ramsey-based engine, heads northwards in about 1965. (Manx Press Pictures)

Passengers enjoyed spectacular scenery on the west coast section near Gob-y-Deigan, but this stretch of the former MNR line caused expensive problems for the IMR because of the frequent fears of subsidence and the instability of embankments. Here, no. 14, *Thornhill*, heads a Ramsey train northwards.

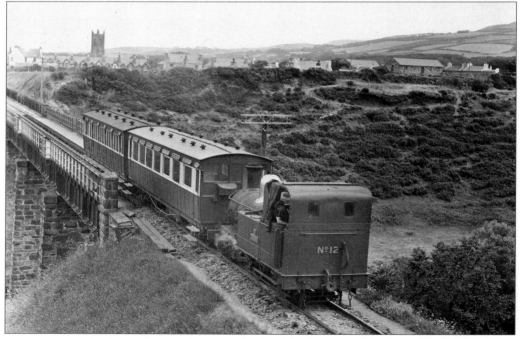

Close to the village of Kirk Michael were the pleasure grounds of Glen Wyllin, purchased and developed by the railway in 1935. The railway crossed the glen by a viaduct, one of two similar engineering structures on this length. Here, locomotive no. 12, *Hutchinson*, crosses the viaduct with a south-bound train in July 1950. (E. Gray)

Winter snowfalls often led to operational difficulties for the railway, mainly because of the problems caused by drifting snow settling and blocking cuttings, particularly on exposed parts of the North Line. Here, no. 11, *Maitland*, fitted front and rear with small snow ploughs, charges a drift in 1965. (Manx Press Pictures)

The small snowplough fitted to *Maitland*'s rear buffer beam is apparent in this view as workers with shovels assist in keeping the line clear for service trains. When the small ploughs proved unable to cope, *Caledonia*, carrying a larger plough, was called into action. The author first saw *Caledonia* in the month of August, when she was stored in the steam shed but still fitted with the large plough, which must have remained in place since her last duty. (Manx Press Pictures)

The terminal area at Ramsey took on a neglected and abandoned air, coming to life only briefly when trains arrived and departed. During the mid-day period, a locomotive on lay-over could be found simmering quietly in the shed, or by the water tank, its absent crew taking refreshment elsewhere. Here, no. 11, *Thornhill*, arrives back on its home ground in 1959. (Dr R.P. Hendry)

The main running line to Ramsey ended alongside a canopied platform by the station building. A train with a mixture of carriages has been assembled in the bay platform by locomotives 8 and 12, which appear ready to depart. In later years, long trains were unusual for the Ramsey line except on occasions of special movements. (RAS Marketing)

Behind the carriage shed at Ramsey lay the weighbridge, water tower, and coaling platform, where *Fenella* rests during a mid-day layover in June 1965. The author's first ride on the Isle of Man railway was from Ramsey behind *Fenella*, and the abiding memory is of the little engine setting off at a cracking pace, whistling to alert the crossing-keepers as she raced along the North Line. (E. Gray)

In 1882–3 a connecting track was laid from the northernmost siding at Ramsey, through a gateway in the walled yard and along the west quay. The harbour tramway enabled the direct discharge of imports and exports from ship to rail, or vice versa. The extension was worked as required when boats arrived, latterly bringing in fuel for the railway until 1949. Here, no. 1, *Sutherland*, hauls a rake of loaded wagons from the quayside in 1938. (G. Harrop)

ISLE OF MAN RAILWAY CO.

To Visitors by this Steamer.

WHERE TO GO

ON

ARRIVAL at DOUGLAS.

☞ The **Isle of Man Railway** takes you **Quickly, Comfortably** and **Cheaply** to—

Train Service :

3rd Return		
Port Erin 2/4	Douglas dep. 1-45 2-15	pm
Castletown 1/5		Port Erin dep. 4-15
Rushen Abbey 1/6		Castletown ,, 4-34
Including Admission.		Ballasalla ,, 4-41
		Douglas arr. 5- 7
St. John's 1/3		St. John's dep. 4- 8
For Tynwald Hill, &c.	Douglas dep. 2-15 2-45	
Peel - - 1/8		Peel ... ,, 3-55
		Douglas arr. 4-31

Motor Bus Service between Pier and Station.

DOUGLAS STATION—Top End of Harbour, West End of Athol St.

A. M. SHEARD, Asst. Sec. & Manager.

Printed at "Herald" Office, Douglas.

The location of Douglas station, at the far end of the inner harbour, was not immediately obvious to newcomers arriving by boat. In an attempt to attract more custom, A.M. Sheard (Manager, 1926–65) prepared handbills to be distributed to passengers disembarking from certain arrivals, and offered a motor bus service from pier to station.

For a short distance beyond Douglas station, the South Line ran alongside the Peel line before curving off to commence the steep climb through the rhododendron bushes of the damp Nunnery cutting. Locomotives accelerated smartly from the station precincts in order to gain momentum to tackle the gradient. Here, no. 10, *G.H. Wood*, works hard on the ascent in July 1965. (Manx Press Pictures)

Locomotive no. 4, *Loch*, heads a South Line train over the stone arched Kewaigue bridge in May 1985. On the nationalisation of the railway, control passed to the Manx Electric Railway Board, which had been government-owned since 1957. The title 'Isle of Man Railways' was applied to the centre panel of some coaches in 1978. (E. Gray)

A South Line train hauled by no. 11, *Maitland*, displays a mixture of livery styles not uncommon in 1986. Behind the engine is F 67 in all-red. This is one of the coaches created by mounting pairs of former 4-wheel bodies on bogie underframes. Next is a coach painted in the colours later generally adopted (described as purple lake and white), while the remaining three are red with cream window panels. (E. Gray)

Emerging from the cutting as it approaches the summit near Keristal is an afternoon train headed by no. 12, *Hutchinson*. Soon after this point, passengers have a brief glimpse of the sea before the line turns inland to reach Port Soderick station. In 1981 this locomotive had been reboilered, given an enlarged cab, and painted royal blue. It is seen here in this modified form. (E. Gray)

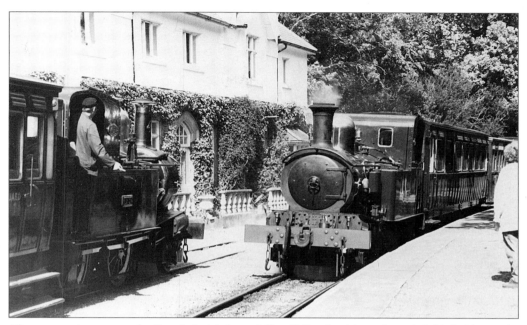

Afternoon trains pass on the Port Soderick loop. Jeffrey Kelly, the driver of no. 4 (left), holds out the single-line staff to be accepted by the Port Erin train (no. 10), which had been waiting at the platform for the arrival of the Douglas-bound train. The substantial station building was erected in 1896 and in 1984, having been unused for some years, was offered for sale for £15,000. (E. Gray)

A south-bound train, headed by no. 12, *Hutchinson*, passes through Crogga woods. Here, the waiting photographer can enjoy the peace and tranquillity of a spring or summer afternoon until the sound of a distant whistle announces the train's departure from Port Soderick. The beat of the engine's exhaust grows louder as the train approaches, then fades as it passes and silence is restored. (E. Gray)

Emerging from Crogga woods, the train enters a cutting as it passes beneath a small road bridge at Ballacostain. This was formerly the site of the diminutive 'Rifle Range Halt' which was used at one time by officer cadets from King William's College en route to the shooting range at Pistol Castle. Here, engine no. 4, *Loch*, heads a mixed-livery train in May 1985. (E. Gray)

After Port Soderick, the next loop on the South Line is at Santon station, now relegated to the status of a request halt. Trains do not normally pass here, except on special workings, and the north-side section of the loop is used by trains in both directions. The siding to the right led to the goods platform and cattle dock. (E. Gray)

At the west end of Santon loop the tracks converge to pass under a stone arched bridge which carries the main Douglas–Castletown road. A high embankment then carries the line over the Santon burn on the way to the next station at Ballasalla. Here, locomotives 10 and 11 double-head a Port Erin–Douglas train on the Santon embankment. (E. Gray)

Most South Line trains are scheduled to pass on the station loops at either Ballasalla or Castletown, and here, a south-bound train hauled by locomotive no. 4, *Loch*, waits at the latter. Unusually, the engine (Port Erin-based at this time) had been turned to work chimney-first to Douglas. Castletown, one time capital of the island, is the most important intermediate station, and the provision of platforms is one of several planned improvements. (E. Gray)

Ballabeg, looking west towards Colby, 1972. This former (and little used) request halt on the straight between Castletown and Colby was reached by a sloping path leading from the road bridge in the distance. For years the site was marked only by a platelayer's hut. (E. Gray)

In 1987 the platelayer's hut at Ballabeg was upgraded and had a small verandah added, making it a most attractive country halt, offering a little shelter for the occasional traveller. Here, no. 12, *Hutchinson*, after its 1981 rebuilding, displays its enlarged cab and blue livery as it hauls a Douglas-bound train past the refurbished structure. (E. Gray)

Senior driver John Elkin looks out from the cab of no. 10 as a Port Erin train passes cautiously through the loop at Colby, which, though lacking platforms, has a wooden shelter for the few waiting passengers. The station's busiest time is usually when schoolchildren are returning home from Castletown on the afternoon train. (E. Gray)

Between Colby and Port St Mary lies a length of track on which there are several crossing-gates. The Ballagawne gatehouse, originally tiny like the others, was extended in 1942 to offer spartan living accommodation for the crossing-keeper. At the time of the photograph, the elderly keeper lived elsewhere, and arrived by bicycle when required. (E. Gray)

Port Erin, the terminus of the South Line. Here, no. 11, *Maitland*, still fitted with a small snowplough from its winter duties, stands at the platform with bogie coach F44, a composite vehicle supplied in 1908, comprising third class accommodation with generous luggage van and guard's brake compartment at one end. (Manx Press Pictures)

Proving that it sometimes snows even in Port Erin is no. 15, *Caledonia*, on snow clearance duties with the large snowplough. The worker with the shovel is removing accumulated snow from the front buffer beam. In the background are the locomotive and goods sheds. (Manx Press Pictures)

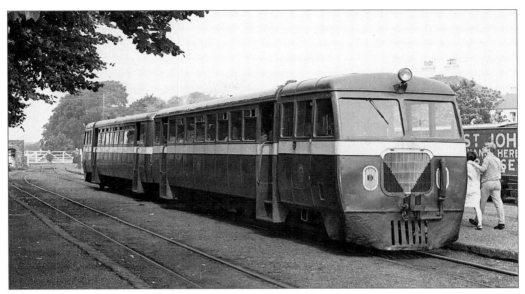

In 1961, with the hope of economising on out-of-season workings, the Company purchased two diesel railcars from the closed County Donegal Railways. These were nos 19 and 20, dating from 1950–1. Arranged back-to-back, they were tested and deemed unsuitable for the South Line, although they could manage the Peel line satisfactorily. (Manx Press Pictures)

Regular passenger services on the Foxdale line ceased in 1940, but mineral trains continued to remove spoil from the waste tips for the construction of airfields in the north of the island. This work ended in 1943, and thereafter there were only occasional trains up to 1945. The line remained intact, though neglected. In 1972 the Foxdale line station at St John's, then a dwelling house, was fronted by overgrown tracks and abandoned wagons. (E. Gray)

Foxdale, 1972. No trains had passed along the line for many years, but the track to Foxdale remained *in situ*, and apparently weed-free because of the use of lead spoil for ballast. In the distance are the Foxdale waste tips, the 'deads', subject of a suggestion in 1963 that in the interests of tourism the line should be re-opened to clear the unsightly mounds. A locomotive last negotiated the long-disused track to Foxdale in 1960. (E. Gray)

The railway closed completely in the autumn of 1965, lay dormant in 1966, and was revived temporarily when leased by the Marquis of Ailsa in 1967. The reprieve proved only partial, and passenger services to Peel and Ramsey ceased in 1968. An engineering train last worked over the closed lines to Ramsey in October 1969. Vegetation soon encroached upon the track – the Peel and Ramsey lines are seen here on the approach to St John's, with the junction to the Foxdale railway on the left. Compare this view with the upper picture on page 16. (E. Gray)

After 1968 the St John's station area took on a desolate and neglected appearance. The track layout remained intact, but derelict 4-wheel carriage bodies, which had served as platform shelters, seemed to add to the atmosphere of decay. George Crellin, that most genial and helpful stationmaster, purchased the former MNR St John's Foxdale line station building, in which he had lived for some time. (E. Gray)

Elsewhere on the North Line, the track had all but disappeared under a lush carpet of vegetation. Sulby Glen station differed from others along this stretch in having a raised platform and canopy, but, like the others on the closed lines at this date, it remained empty and abandoned, awaiting eventual sale for conversion into a dwelling house. The wooden hut (right) was the MNR goods shed of 1885, still carrying remarkably long-lived advertisements. (E. Gray)

On 1 July 1973 celebrations were held to mark the centenary of the opening of the Isle of Man Railway to Peel. As the Peel line was closed, the celebrations took place on the South Line. A ten-coach train, carrying the Governor and other notables, was scheduled to run at 3.45 p.m. non-stop from Port Erin to Douglas. No. 13, *Kissack*, headed the train and carried a special headboard. (E. Gray)

The centenary train was banked in the rear by no. 10, *G.H. Wood*, which also carried a special headboard. Engineman Jeffrey Kelly talks to two guests in period costume prior to departure. Despite the stated intention to run non-stop, the train halted at all stations so that local commissioners could meet the Governor. Consequently, it arrived in Douglas very late. (E. Gray)

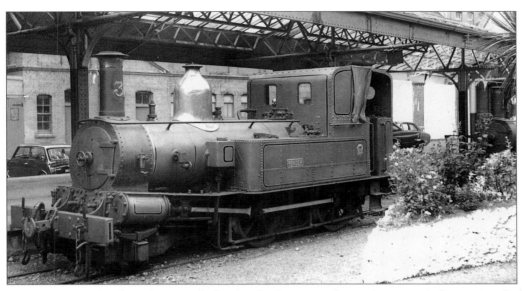

On the centenary day, disused engines displayed at the former North Line departure platform at Douglas included no. 3, *Pender*. No provision was made for the well-wishers and supporters of the railway. Crowds waiting for the (by then very late) centenary train were suddenly and officiously ordered from assorted vantage points and herded to a distant spot away from the arrival platform, causing some to leave in disgust. The locomotive superintendent of the time did not encourage interest in the railway. (E. Gray)

Hopes of re-opening the North Line faded when contractors lifted the track in 1974–5. Worse was to follow, with operation of a shortened South Line in 1975–6, the sale or destruction of unused rolling stock, and the dismantling of Douglas station canopies. Locomotive no. 6 was offered to the National Railway Museum in York, and no. 3 was sold to the Museum of Science & Industry, Manchester, to become a 'sectioned' exhibit – an act of premeditated vandalism, whose stated aim could have been better achieved with a working diagram. (E. Gray)

Affairs seemed marginally brighter with the reboilering of locomotives 11 and 12 in 1981. It was at this time that no. 12, *Hutchinson*, was rebuilt with a larger cab, but not everyone appreciated the fairground image attached to its new blue livery. Someone had decided that it would be a good idea to have all the locomotives in different colours. A new station building at Ballasalla in 1986 resulted only from the sale of the goods yard to developers. (E. Gray)

The future of the railway was by no means assured. At Douglas, motor bus parking and garaging had been allowed to encroach on to the site. Station buildings had been sold or leased. Items slowly deteriorating in the decrepit carriage shed included locomotives 6 *Peveril* and 5 *Mona*, together with other engines and unusable stock. Much goodwill had been lost, and one wondered if the railway could survive. (E. Gray)

DOUGLAS STREET TRAMWAYS

The construction of the Victoria Pier at Douglas in 1872 (and extended 1891) enabled steamers to berth at any state of the tide, and led to an immediate increase in the number of visitors, many of whom were accommodated in hotels built on the new promenade which was to bear Governor Loch's name in 1875. The first portion of the sea-front Douglas Bay Tramway was opened in August 1876 by Thomas Lightfoot, using three horse-drawn tramcars. As with the 1873 railway, a gauge of 3 ft was chosen. At first, the new line was merely single track with passing loops. It was soon extended to a terminus close to the harbour, and after its sale in 1882 to The Isle of Man Tramways Limited, further loops were installed, and an extension made northwards to Derby Castle. In 1894 the tramway passed into the ownership of the Douglas & Laxey Coast Electric Tramway Company, which became the Isle of Man Tramways & Electric Power Company. In 1896 this company also constructed the Upper Douglas cable tramway, an enterprise encouraged by the civic authorities in order to provide public transport for the hilly section of the town. After the bankruptcy of the owning company, Douglas Corporation purchased both tramways in 1902. The cable car system operated only seasonally after 1921, and closed in 1929, a victim of high running costs and motor bus competition, but the horse-trams continue, though usually reduced to a four-car summer service.

For passengers arriving by steamer at the Victoria Pier there was a choice of two methods of horse-drawn transport. Lined up on the right are carriages waiting to carry the wealthier visitors to railway station or hotel. On the left a horse-tram of the open 'toastrack' variety stands at the terminus of the promenade line. Above its running board is the legend TO AND FROM THE MANX ELECTRIC RAILWAY.

For the opening of his horse-tramway in 1876, Thomas Lightfoot ordered one single-deck and two double-deck cars from the Starbuck Company of Birkenhead. Double-deck tramcar no. 4 was supplied by the same firm in 1882, and is seen here after sale to The Isle Of Man Tramways Limited, whose title it carries. The double-deck cars could seat 32: 16 inside and 16 on the top-deck 'knifeboard' seat. By 1891 there were twenty-six cars in service.

The choice of cable-hauled tramcars for the Upper Douglas district was necessitated by the hilly nature of the route. A continuously moving cable, powered from an engine house, ran on pulleys in a conduit beneath the 3 ft gauge tracks. The motorman operated a gripping mechanism via the centre slot to hold or release the cable. The track and centre slot in Victoria Street are seen here before the reinstatement of the road surface. Services began in August 1896. (Manx National Heritage)

The terminus of the cable car line was at the seaward end of Victoria Street, close to the horse-tramway at the 1887 Jubilee Clock. One of the open-ended cable cars of the 79–82 series stands at the terminus (left), while an open 'toastrack' car waits to reverse on Loch Promenade. Horse-tram 32 has just commenced its journey and passes no. 20, the latter being one of the small 'toastracks' identifiable by the arched end irons carrying the lamps.

The terminal spur of the cable car route in Victoria Street was linked to the horse-tramway by a connecting track, seen in the foreground. Under Douglas Corporation ownership, the tramway was extended on to the Victoria Pier, and in 1905 a short shuttle service was introduced to convey people from the steamer berths to the cable car terminus in Victoria Street. (David Bailey collection)

Cable tram no. 72 climbing Prospect Hill. Cable car numbers began at 71 so as not to conflict with any possible increase in the 37-strong horse-tram fleet in 1896, though later additions in 1907–9 were allocated the numbers 67–70 in descending order. The original 2-mile route passed from Victoria Street via Bucks Road, Woodbourne Road, and York Road back to the promenade at Broadway. Fares to Murray's Road were one penny up, twopence down. (S.R. Keig/Manx National Heritage)

Cable car no. 73 at Salisbury Terrace ready to return southwards to Victoria Street. A crossover for short workings lies beyond the car, just short of the sharp right turn at Avondale into York Road. As early as 1902, the Ballaquayle Road–Broadway single-track portion of the service was abandoned, the route being curtailed because of the difficulty of working the last steep and narrow section. (Manx National Heritage)

This 1920 postcard shows cable car no. 78 by the Jubilee Clock as two covered 'toastracks' pass on the promenade service. A notice on the base of the clock informs potential travellers that the 'Last Car Leaves at 11.20 p.m.' The grand sweep of period architecture, so impressive to arriving visitors, has now been lost by the destruction of the Villiers Hotel section and its replacement by a new office block. (Valentine)

This mid-1920s view of the Loch Promenade includes an early motor lorry and one of the 'sunshade' 'toastrack' cars (nos 22–24). New in 1890–1, these three cars were fitted with ridged canvas roofs in about 1908. The awnings, stretched over metal frames, could be rolled back if required. Holiday-makers peer over the railings at the high tide. (Valentine)

Moving northwards around the bay from Loch Promenade, the next length is the Harris Promenade, where horse-tram no. 34 is passing one of the double-deck vehicles as it moves towards the Villa Marina in about 1924. The tram stop sign is affixed to the lamp-post in the middle of the road and bears the legend WAIT HERE FOR HORSE TRAMS. (Valentine)

Central Promenade and Shore from Villa Marina, Douglas, I.O.M. 203027 J

Beyond the Villa Marina the title changes to Central Promenade. By the Cabin Café, on the left in this 1927 picture, is the junction with Broadway. In 1896 the Broadway terminus of the cable car route was only a few yards from the horse-tram track, but the two were not connected at this point. The Broadway section of the cable route was abandoned in 1902 because of difficulties in operating the steep incline on narrow streets. (Valentine)

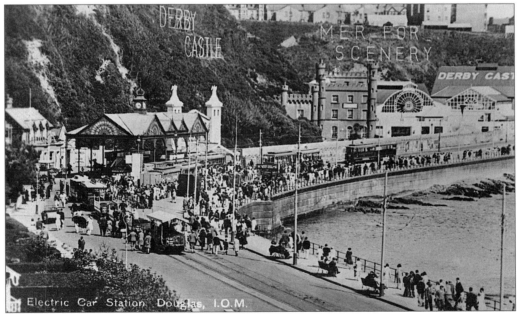

Electric Car Station Douglas, I.O.M.

At the north end of the promenade, the horse-tramway had been extended in 1890 to terminate at Derby Castle. When the electric tramway opened in 1893, the termini were only a few yards apart on adjacent, though unconnected, tracks. The splendid cast-iron canopy was erected in 1896, at which time both tramways were owned by the Isle of Man Tramways & Electric Power Company. Horse-tram fares along the promenade were twopence each way.

Fleet numbers of the horse-tramcars reached 50 by 1935, but the closed single-decker outside the Strathallan Crescent depot was the second vehicle to carry the number 1. It was obtained in 1913 from the Milnes Voss Company. The closed cars are used in poor weather, their half-vestibule offering partial protection for the driver. (Roy Brook)

Cars 34, 21, 50, and 1 stand on the track fan outside the depot. Car 50 was the last of three 'all-weather' cars purchased in 1935 from the Vulcan Engineering Company. The side-screens could be folded away or left in place, according to weather conditions. The offices above the depot were added in 1935, and are now the headquarters of Isle of Man Transport.

A traverser, running sideways on tracks laid across the depot access lines, offers a method of car delivery or collection to or from any particular line in the depot. Car 10, sitting on the traverser in 1981, was one of the first open 'toastracks'. It had been lengthened in 1935, and later given end-posts for the advertising boards. Now sadly lost, it dated from 1884 and was the oldest original survivor in the fleet. (E. Gray)

Car 12, supplied by G.F. Milnes in 1888, is a 32-seat eight-bench open car, the sole survivor of the small 'toastrack' series, now used only on special occasions. Its iron arches carry lamp houses. The heavier double-deck cars remained largely unused in post-war years. The present fleet comprises twenty-three vehicles, only one of which is double-deck. (E. Gray)

Double-deck horse-tram no. 18 has a complex history. It arrived in the Isle of Man in 1887, one of six vehicles purchased second-hand from a closed tramway at South Shields. In about 1906 it was converted to a single-deck car, but in 1989–90 it was returned to its original double-deck condition. The only other double-deck survivor is a static exhibit in the Manx Museum. (E. Gray)

The cable tramway closed in August 1929 to be replaced by a motor bus service. The cars were sold off cheaply for other uses. In 1968 nos 72 and 73 were rescued from their role as a bungalow in the north of the island. Keith Pearson and his team used the best parts of each to create one restored vehicle, numbered 72 at one end, 73 at the other. It is exhibited in the horse-tram depot. (E. Gray)

THE MANX ELECTRIC RAILWAY

The Manx Electric Railway originated in a scheme to build a road from the north end of Douglas promenade to Ramsey. Powers were granted to construct a 3 ft gauge railway along the course of the road, and capital was raised by promoter Alexander Bruce. By September 1893 a single line was completed as far as Groudle, and services were run for a few days until the end of the season. Work then commenced on the northward extension to Laxey, the company adopting the title 'Douglas & Laxey Coast Electric Tramway'. The starting point of the line was 2 miles away from the steamer berths, so the 1894 purchase of the Douglas horse-tramway was seen as a vital step towards future conversion to electric operation along the promenade to Victoria Pier. (This ambition was subsequently frustrated by objections from hoteliers, cab-owners, and those who did not approve of unsightly overhead wires.) With Alexander Bruce as Chairman, the combined undertaking 'The Isle of Man Tramways & Electric Power Company' also constructed the Upper Douglas cable tramway in 1896. The electric tramway reached the outskirts of Ramsey in 1898, and was extended to the present terminus in 1899.

The failure of Dumbell's Bank in 1900, of which Bruce was General Manager, was due in part to underestimating the cost of constructing the Ramsey line, and led to the bankruptcy of the Company. In 1902 Douglas Corporation bought the horse and cable lines, while the electric tramway passed to the Manx Electric Railway Company. Fifty years on, the failing tourist trade aroused fears of closure, but a campaign to save the line led to a government take-over in 1957. The line did, in fact, close in 1975, with seasonal operation only on the Douglas–Laxey section. Happily, the full service to Ramsey resumed in June 1977.

For the opening of the service on the new line to Groudle in 1893, the Birkenhead firm of G.F. Milnes supplied three open-platform cars, seating 38, and six open trailer cars, seating 44. It was hoped that each power car would be able to haul two trailers. Car 3 and trailer 16 are seen on test on the then single track by the uncompleted road overlooking Port Groudle. (Weir Pumps/Mather & Platt)

The six 1893 trailers (thought to be nos 11–16 originally, but renumbered several times as the power car fleet grew) were soon fitted with side pillars to support light roofs. Trailer 15 is seen behind one of the 1894 vestibuled saloon cars (nos 4–9) at the Derby Castle terminus ready to commence a northward journey. (Weir Pumps/Mather & Platt)

Land reclaimed from the Port-e-Varda creek, just a few yards north of Derby Castle, provided a site for the construction of the electric car depot and power house. Cars 6 and 3 stand in the original No. 1 shed of 1893. Electrical equipment was supplied by Mather & Platt of Salford. The cars drew current from the overhead wire via bow collectors patented by Edward Hopkinson, a director of Mather & Platt. (Weir Pumps/Mather & Platt)

The 1893 limit of the line was outside the Groudle Glen Hotel. The glen at that time was being developed as a major tourist attraction, and there was considerable seasonal traffic from Douglas. Car 9 with trailer has just negotiated the crossover and stands ready to return to Douglas.

The interior of car 1 is a splendid example of the Victorian coachbuilder's skill. The wooden body is beautifully preserved. Strips of carpet laid along the seats offer little in the way of comfort to today's passengers, but the experience of riding in an 1893 vehicle, now the oldest electric tramcar operating on its original line, cannot be matched anywhere else in the world. (E. Gray)

A commemorative photograph of the first passenger working to Laxey, 28 July 1894. Trailer 19 was one of six additional trailers (originally numbered 17–22) supplied by Milnes in 1894. Unlike the first trailers, the second batch came complete with wooden roof and end bulkheads. It is drawn by one of the 1894 saloon cars (nos 4–9) on the sharp curve at Groudle. (Weir Pumps/Mather & Platt)

The 1894 temporary terminus at Laxey lay just short of the Rencell Road cutting, which was not bridged until the following year. Car 2, hauling a lightweight trailer, stands on the cross-over track. Off the picture to the left is the site of the future depot. The fare from Derby Castle to Laxey was one shilling. (Weir Pumps/Mather & Platt)

Car 3 returning to Douglas on the long climb from Laxey to South Cape. While cars 1 and 2 survive to this day, car 3 was lost in 1930 (along with cars 4, 8, and 24, and several trailers) in a disastrous fire at the Laxey Car Shed. (Weir Pumps/Mather & Platt)

Four additional power cars (nos 10–13) were obtained from G.F. Milnes in 1895. They had unglazed sides and were built to rather spartan specifications, so they enjoyed but a brief existence as passenger cars. Two were withdrawn as early as 1902 and the other two were converted for freight traffic. No. 11 is seen here at Groudle in 1895. (David Bailey collection)

The Hopkinson bow collectors proved unreliable in service, and in 1897 a decision was taken to re-equip the cars to collect current by means of the pole and trolley-wheel system. The roof-top fittings were changed and the entire overhead between Douglas and Laxey was replaced and re-hung. Car 3, bearing the 1902 title, stands by the depot entrance. (David Bailey collection)

Car 13, shown re-equipped with trolley pole, prepares for a return journey from Groudle in about 1900. Power cars manoeuvre round their trailers by uncoupling, moving forward, then reversing out of the way via the cross-over while the trailer is shunted past the points by gravity or manpower. Car 13 is about to reverse once again to couple up ready for the return journey. (David Bailey collection)

IMPORTANT ANNOUNCEMENT!

THIS IS
GLORIOUS WEATHER!!
FOR THE
OPEN ELECTRIC CARS
TO
Laxey, Snaefell Summit, and Ramsey.

Health-giving Sea and Mountain Breezes.
and NO DUST.

16 Miles of CHARMING SCENERY, from Sea Level to 2,000 feet of altitude.

The ELECTRIC CARS run from
DERBY CASTLE
EVERY FEW MINUTES.

The Manx Electric Railway Co., Ltd., Strathallan Crescent, Douglas.

HAROLD BROWN, General Manager.

Brown & Sons, Ltd., Printers, Douglas.

This handbill from the 1900s, when Harold Brown was manager, advertises health-giving breezes and no dust!

The attractions of the coastal ride to Laxey and Ramsey, and the ascent of Snaefell, brought holiday season crowds in huge numbers to board the electric cars at Derby Castle. In this 1904 postcard view, trams line up on the seaward track, waiting to collect their quota of passengers. Nearest the camera is trailer 51 coupled to a 1–3 series car, and the next trailer is number 34.

The proximity of the horse and electric tramways at Derby Castle is well illustrated in this busy scene. In the foreground, horse-tram 24, departing southwards, advertises Laxey Glen gardens, while trailer 56 waits at the end of the electric line. The splendid ornate canopy erected in 1896 spanned the horse-tram terminus. The return fare to Ramsey, or Snaefell summit, was two shillings and sixpence.

On a wet day in 1962, car 6 propels its trailer to the terminal track. The shutters of the trailer car are pulled down as protection from the weather. In such conditions, the great canopy (demolished 1980) provided useful shelter for passengers of both horse- and electric tramways. A large board along the seaward side was used to advertise the presence of the tramway. (E. Gray)

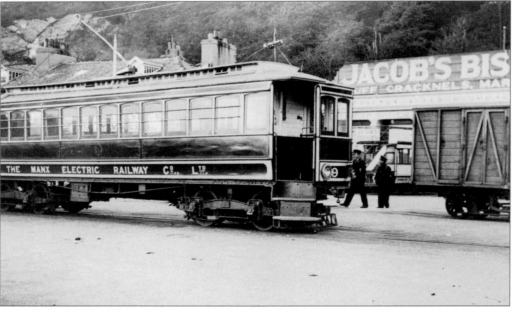

Car 9, displaying the full company title, stands at the end of the track at Derby Castle. Goods van 15 is parked on the adjacent line, and beyond is the Strathallan Crescent horse-tram depot, to which an upper storey was added in 1935. This upper portion is now the administration centre for Isle of Man Transport. (David Bailey collection)

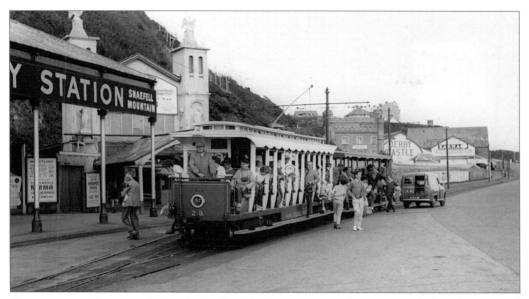

Passengers travelling outwards from Derby Castle in the mornings tend to return in the late afternoon and extra car sets wait at Laxey to bring returning holiday-makers home from Snaefell. Here, crossbench car 29 of 1904 brings its well-loaded trailer to a halt in 1962. The ratchet cars, lacking air brakes, are little used today. Car 29 has been in store for over twenty-five years. (E. Gray)

Derby Castle depot yard track layout seen from above, 1972. The three-road No. 1 car shed is bottom right; other sheds (centre left) were added in stages between 1894 and 1896, and shed 5 in 1924. Crossbench car 27 and two goods vans stand on the southernmost track, while a car of the 5–9 series waits at the seaward side. (E. Gray)

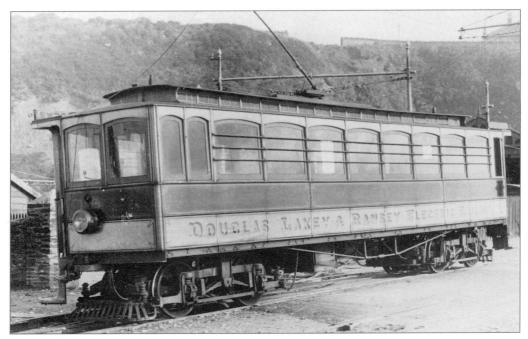

In 1899 G.F. Milnes supplied four fully enclosed 'winter saloons' (nos 19–22), which have proved to be the most intensively used cars in both winter and summer. An exchange of equipment took place in 1904, by which these four cars gained the trucks and air brake fittings from recently arrived cars 28–31. Car 19 stands at the depot entrance, bearing the title applied in about 1900, and looking badly in need of a re-paint. (David Bailey collection)

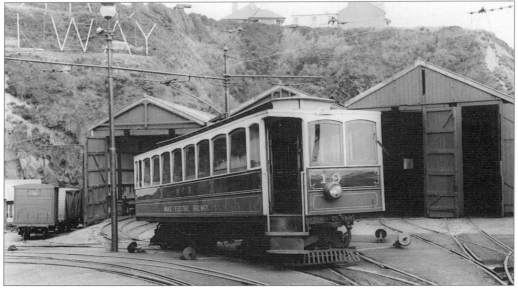

Sixty-five years on, and car 19 waits the call of duty on the track fan in front of the top sheds in the depot yard. Goods vans are parked on the former Bonner Wagon siding by No. 2 shed. At this date, car 19 displayed 'M.E.R.' on the panel beneath the windows, and 'Manx Electric Railway' in full on the lower panel. Cars 19–22 gained upholstered seats in 1932. (E. Gray)

Inside the three-track No. 1 shed in 1965 cars 1 and 30 (centre) stand over the inspection pits, while other crossbench vehicles are parked on the right. The 'hospital roads' are so-called because they are used to store vehicles needing repair or attention of some sort. The trolley wires run in the wooden troughing above each road. Car 30 has been stored out of use at Laxey for many years. (E. Gray)

Shed No. 2 was built in 1894–5. On the wall (left) are hung a number of coupling bars. Because of the differences in height between various classes of towing car and trailer, several of the bars are cranked to match different combinations, usually designated by marking the appropriate bar with the suitable fleet numbers. (E. Gray)

Shed No. 3 was an 1895–6 sideways extension of shed 2. The piecemeal growth of the depot complex was evidenced by the roof profile and different floor levels between the various sections. The timber frames show up well in this 1972 view. The floors were a compacted mass of earth and grease. Car 31 is in shed 3, while car 15 can be seen beyond in shed 2. (E. Gray)

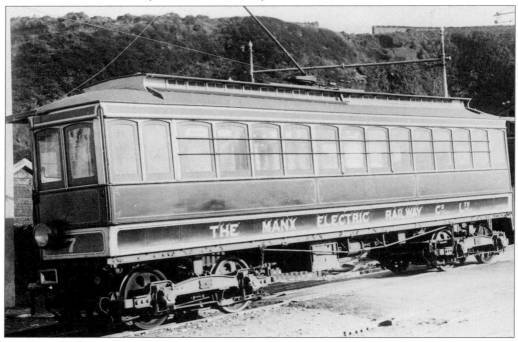

Car 7 of 1895 stands on the landward running line at the entrance to Derby Castle sheds. It carries the 1902 Company's title, which was painted along the red rocker panel in white letters shaded in black. The new company bought much new equipment to improve performance, including the new Brush type trucks for the 5–9 series to replace the originals. The security rails were removed when the sash windows were altered to half-drop. (David Bailey collection)

In June 1972 ratchet car 17 was operating without trailer on the Onchan shuttle service, and is seen here coasting down the slope from Port Jack as it returns to Douglas. Six years later, after a change of manager, and at a time when items from the steam railway were being sold off, this was one of four crossbench cars (15, 17, 28 and 31) and four trailers (50, 51, 53 and 54) for which offers were invited. (E. Gray)

The first busy crossing at the start of the northward journey is at Port Jack, where the tramway crosses the road junction on an uphill curve. In 1979 some cars emerging from overhaul appeared in mock 'historic' liveries. Car 21, one of the four winter saloons, displays a version of the 'Douglas, Laxey, & Ramsey Electric Railway' livery of 1900, as it climbs past Port Jack in 1985. (E. Gray)

The 10–13 series cars were similar to the Snaefell Mountain Tramway cars supplied by Milnes in the same year, 1895. They were the last to carry Mather & Platt electrical equipment. The body style developed from that of the 4–9 series, but transverse seats replaced the longitudinal benches of the earlier vehicles. Car 12 is pictured at the Groudle Tram station in about 1902 during its short life as a passenger car.

The four cars of the 10–13 class, having a more austere body design, were withdrawn from passenger service by the new management in about 1902. Car 12 was stripped of its seats and in 1903 appeared in a new guise as a motor cattle truck. Another was converted to a motorised goods vehicle, and the other two were kept in store until 1918, when they emerged as freight trailers.

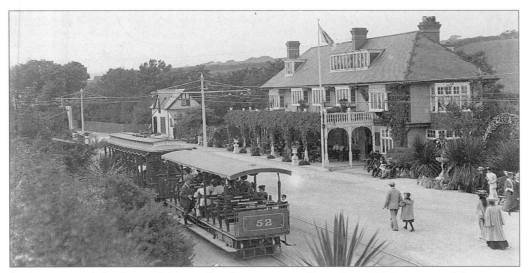

Trailer 52, seen behind one of the crossbench cars at Groudle in about 1906, was one of the six open
trailers supplied in 1893 as nos 11–16. The light wooden roof was a later addition and, later still, end
bulkheads were fitted. In recent years, no. 52, with seats, roof, and one dash panel removed, has been
used as a rail carrier for the permanent way department.

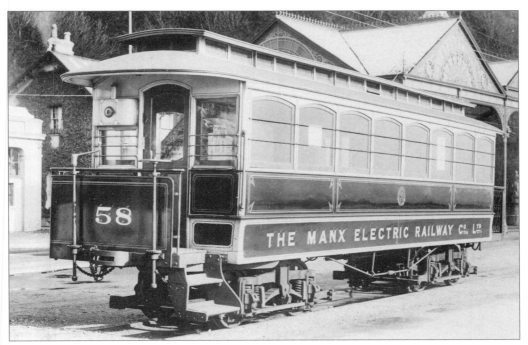

Winter traffic in the early years was such that two of the closed power cars had been used as saloon
trailers. In order to avoid this wasteful use of vehicles, two 'winter trailers' (57–58) were supplied in
1904 by the Electric Railway & Tramway Carriage Company of Preston. The entrance steps are arranged
on the 'wrong side' to coincide with those of the towing car, and enable the conductor to move from one
vehicle to the other. (David Bailey collection)

The tramway company gained much revenue from the carriage of goods, parcels and mail, and so acquired a considerable number of freight vehicles. A curious development was the 1899 purchase of three Bonner road-rail wagons from Toledo. On the tramway, the wagons were towed on a low truck, which could be withdrawn at the end of the journey to transfer the load to the road wheels.

The tramway company has the distinction of being the first operator of motor coaches on the island. A service was established in 1907 to carry passengers from the Bungalow on the Snaefell tramway to the hotel and tea gardens owned by the company at Tholt-y-Will in Sulby Glen. Two 'Argus' 16-seat charabancs, MN 67 and 68, ran until the outbreak of war in 1914. (Courtesy Terry Faragher)

A succession of road vehicles operated the Tholt-y-Will service over the years. Bedford/Duple coach MN 8874, new in 1933, was one of two second-hand 20-seater vehicles purchased in 1939 just before services ceased for the second time. The service was reinstated when hostilities ended and ran until 1952.

In 1953 coach MN 8874 was converted into a motor van for the goods and parcels service, in which form it continued in use until 1957. It is seen here at the Derby Castle terminus parked alongside car 22. The parcels service ended in 1966 but the contract for collecting mail from the lineside boxes was retained until the 1975–7 closure of the Laxey–Ramsey section. (Roy Brook)

The year is 1930 as car 6 heads northwards through an area now much altered by the spread of urban development. At this date the coast road approaching Howstrake was unsurfaced, but the configuration of the track, where car 6 leans to the bend near Far End, makes the spot recognisable. Cars 6–9 are often referred to as 'tunnel' cars because of their long narrow saloons. (David Bailey collection)

Douglas-bound ratchet car no. 18 negotiates the sharp curve as it leaves the Groudle viaduct. The corrugated iron chalet on the left (now demolished) was formerly the toll house in the days when the road was owned by the tramway company. Of the 1898 Milnes-built 14–18 batch, only car 16 has air brakes (fitted 1902–4) and is in regular use. Of the others, 18 is used sparingly. (E. Gray)

Car 1 towing trailer 47 pauses at Baldrine on its way to Douglas. The shelter, in a pleasant location, is typical of many along the line. Mail from the adjoining GPO letter box was once collected by tramway staff. The original 1899 structure has been refurbished and fitted with an attractive nameboard. (E. Gray)

Car 7 negotiates the road crossing at Baldrine. The end platforms of the 5–9 batch of cars were originally fitted with twin windows divided by a central pillar, but these were replaced by a single pane in 1966–8, with the object of improving driver visibility. However, car 6 has now been restored to original appearance. (E. Gray)

Northbound winter saloon 19 passes the cross-over at Garwick. To the left there used to be a complex of station buildings catering for visitors to Garwick Glen and caves, once a popular beauty spot. The glen became privately owned, and the station was reduced to a small shelter, demolished in 1979. The site is now overgrown, and little trace remains. (E. Gray)

Moving northwards from Garwick towards Laxey, the tramway crosses the main Douglas–Laxey road just south of Ballabeg. Flashing light warning signals on the highway are activated by the approach of a tramcar. Car 18 has been the only ratchet car available for use in recent times. Most are in store in poor condition, and some were cannibalised for parts to keep others in service. (E. Gray)

North of Ballabeg begins the long descent to Laxey. Passengers on this stretch of line gain spectacular views seawards and over Laxey Bay. Here, Douglas-bound winter saloon 22 climbs the gradient from South Cape. (E. Gray)

Car 5 climbing southwards from Laxey halts at the cross-over at Fairy Cottage. It displays the one-piece platform window. Unlike the other cars of this batch, car 5 has transverse seating, fitted in 1932, and also has a partition dividing the compartments of the saloon. It is sometimes referred to as 'The Shrine' or 'The Cathedral' because the interior woodwork is reminiscent of church fittings. (E. Gray)

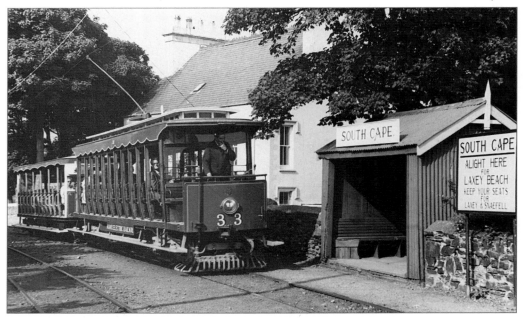

In 1906, with the addition of two power cars (32–33) and two trailers (61–62), supplied by the United Electric Car Company of Preston, the fleet reached its maximum of 33 motor cars (1–33) and 29 trailers (34–62). Car 33 is seen here at South Cape hauling trailer 37. The sign 'Alight here for Laxey Beach. Keep your seats for Laxey and Snaefell' is correct for north-bound travellers only! (E. Gray)

From South Cape the line runs downwards along the southern slope of the Laxey valley. In this 1962 picture, winter saloon 20 climbs the gradient from the village. The line onwards to Ramsey leaves Laxey on the opposite side of the valley. Compare this view with the upper picture on page 64 of car 3 in the same location. (E. Gray)

The depot at Laxey is located some way short of the main station, on land close to the original terminus of the line. It has a long headshunt, on which, at busy summer periods, extra car sets once waited out of the way of service cars until summoned into the station to collect passengers returning from Snaefell. Car 15 with trailer 37 waits in June 1965. (E. Gray)

Car 31, standing outside the Laxey car shed, is one of four crossbench motor cars (28–31) supplied by the United Electric Car Company in 1903. As part of the same order were two matching open trailers (55–56) and two winter saloon trailers (57–58). Car 31 was one of four cars offered for sale by tender in the depressing years around 1978, but it has since been overhauled. (E. Gray)

The main running line passes the north side of Laxey shed, and is reached from the depot via the headshunt and its connecting track (left). A cross-over is provided at the side of the shed. The depot itself has four tracks but, unusually, the fourth, the southernmost track, can be reached only from the back by way of the third track and a (now overgrown) headshunt at the rear. (E. Gray)

The original Laxey Car Shed was destroyed by fire in 1930. Eleven vehicles were lost in the conflagration: cars 3, 4, 8 and 24, and trailers 34–35, 38–41 and 44. Only three were replaced, with trailers built to the 1904 pattern and given numbers 40, 41 and 44. In 1965 goods trailer 26 (ex-motor car 10 of 1895) and the body of the steeple cab locomotive 23, both unused for many years, rested on the southernmost track mentioned above. (E. Gray)

Ramsey-bound car 5 passes the rear of the depot as it approaches the Rencell Road overbridge. This was the site of the first Laxey terminus in 1894, illustrated on page 63. Immediately behind the camera is the Laxey sub-station. Until 1935 the Company generated its own electricity, but has since drawn from the public supply. The sub-stations transform the power to the correct line voltage. (E. Gray)

The approach to Laxey is via the impressive curved four-arch viaduct over Glen Roy, erected in 1898 to bring the line into the new station site. The extension involved the track passing through part of the church grounds to a stopping point in the mine captain's garden. Car 6 crosses the viaduct to enter the station in 1985. (E. Gray)

The new station area at Laxey in the early years of the century. With the extension of the Snaefell tramway to a terminal point in the joint station, Laxey became the hub of the system. A substantial refreshment room (centre, right of car 4) was constructed in 1899. The booking office and waiting room (extreme right, now refurbished), and the sales kiosks survive, but the refreshment rooms were destroyed by fire in 1917.

With the development of the new station site at Laxey, transfer between the Manx Electric and the Snaefell line became easy and convenient. The mountain tramway terminates alongside the northbound track of the coastal line. In 1962 car 16 arrives from Douglas as Snaefell car 2, the latter in the short-lived 'nationalised' livery of green and cream, waits on the terminal stub of the adjoining track. (E. Gray)

At Laxey a sign instructed passengers where to wait for the Snaefell cars, while another invited them to extend their journey 'to Royal Ramsey, passing through the garden of the island'. Ratchet car 28, on an extra working to Laxey, comes to a halt in the summer of 1962, while a car for Douglas departs on the southbound track. (E. Gray)

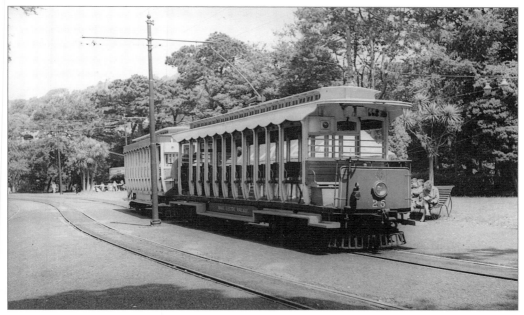

The Douglas–Laxey portion of the line has always been busier than the northern section because of the large numbers of holiday-makers wishing to visit Snaefell or the great Laxey Wheel. Extra workings to and from Laxey are rostered in between the regular service cars to and from Ramsey. Car 25 with trailer 55 waits in 1965 at the departure point for Douglas. (E. Gray)

Laxey station from the north end, 1981. The Snaefell line (right) is six inches wider than the 3 ft gauge coastal tramway. After crossing the Laxey–Ramsey road as single track, it branches into two terminal stubs, one of which is linked to the MER's northbound track (centre) by a dual-gauge siding. Here, car 14, with shutters down while in use by the poles and wires gang, is propelling a tower wagon. (E. Gray)

The former mines captain's house, close to the tracks at the north end of Laxey station, was converted into the Station Hotel, now the Mines Tavern. Car 17, in use by the permanent way department, passes alongside towing an open goods wagon. The use of oil lamps on the dash panels was required by statute to supplement the electric lights until the 1980s. (David Bailey collection)

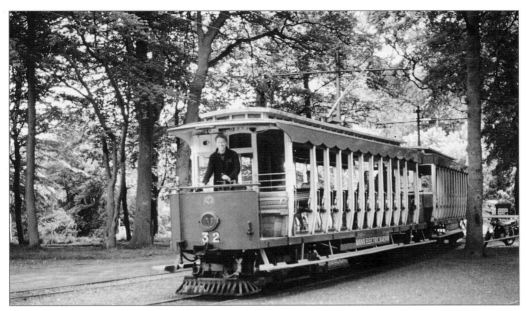

After the nationalisation of the Manx Electric Railway in 1957, the Board decided to discard the traditional colours of red or brown with white or ivory and varnished teak, in favour of a green and white livery. This did not prove popular, and the policy was soon abandoned, but in 1979 car 32 and trailer 61 reappeared in green and white as an example of the short-lived scheme. Laxey 1985. (E. Gray)

From Laxey, the Ramsey line climbs along the far slopes of the valley. Car 16 coasts down the southbound gradient. This car, and the 24–27 series, are known as 'paddleboxes' because of the shape of the footboards, altered in 1902–4 to accommodate the axleboxes of the wider Brush trucks. In the valley bottom (right) were formerly the mines' washing floors and mineral tramway. (E. Gray)

Car 33 hauling trailer 37 is driven by motorman Mike Goodwyn (Chairman of the Manx Electric Railway Society and noted writer on transport topics) as it passes over the viaduct at Minorca, where there is a small shelter for waiting passengers. Cars 32 and 33 of 1906, the youngest and most powerful vehicles in the fleet, are in regular use each season. (E. Gray)

Climbing onwards from Minorca the line hugs the cliff tops. Passengers who travel no further than Laxey miss the spectacular scenery on the northern section of the line. Car 19 with trailer 40 coasts down the southbound track near Bulgham Bay. The collapse of part of the embankment wall at Bulgham in 1967 interrupted through services for over a year. (E. Gray)

The summit of the line, 588 ft above sea level, is reached some 2½ miles north of Laxey. Paddlebox 27, towing a tower wagon, has just negotiated the sharp bend near the summit as it begins the southward drop into Laxey. Car 27, used as the engineering car for some years, had been called out to attend to an overhead line repair. (E. Gray)

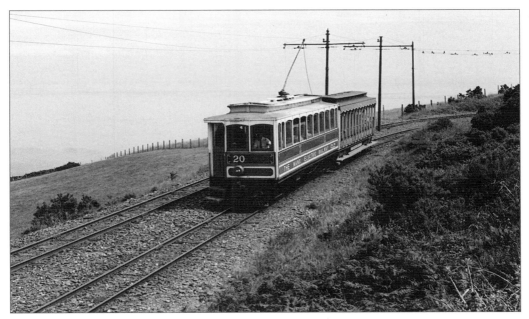

From the northern side of the sharp curve at Ballaragh summit, there are splendid views over Dhoon Bay towards Maughold Head. Here, the line begins to fall towards the next stopping place at the head of Dhoon Glen. Winter saloon 20, on the regular service to Ramsey, emerges from the curve to join the straight alongside the glen. (E. Gray)

This official Manx Electric Railway postcard shows the large hotel and refreshment room which once existed opposite the tramway station at Dhoon Glen. Sadly, the hotel was destroyed by fire in 1932 and the site is now a convenient car park for visitors to the glen. Crossbench car 17 is on the southward track, as a car set with goods van attached passes northwards.

The trees around the Dhoon Glen station have grown considerably since the date of the previous illustration. The present shelter, dating from 1987, replaced an older version. Behind it is a small refreshment room. Paddlebox 26, with motorman Bob Clarke, pauses on its journey from Ramsey. The 24–27 series of cars were originally trailers, motorised by the line's new owners after 1902. (E. Gray)

The tramway was once an important carrier of stone produced in the associated quarries at Dhoon and Ballajora. At Dhoon there was an extensive layout with a loading dock and weighbridge. Sidings were fed by an aerial ropeway and narrow gauge tramway. In 1972 the cut-down remains of a former freight car rested on a siding, apparently abandoned, but it was subsequently rescued and adapted as a track repair unit. (E. Gray)

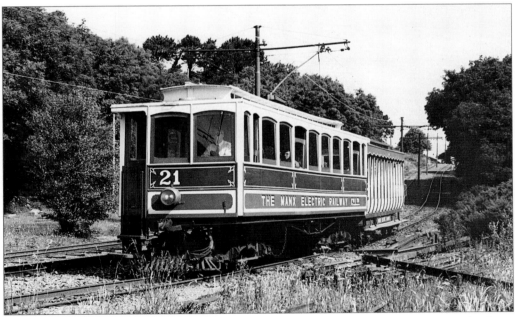

Stone traffic has long since ceased, and in recent years Dhoon Quarry sidings have been utilised as a convenient repository for permanent way materials. Half buried in the long grass, right, are piles of steel rails, as winter saloon 21 and trailer 44 hurry past on the first journey of the day from Ramsey to Douglas. (E. Gray)

Along the course of the line are numerous minor road and farm crossings, on the approach to which a warning air-whistle, sounded by a small foot-operated button on the driving platform, heralds the tram's proximity. The ratchet cars, lacking air-operated equipment, rely on the sound of the traditional gong. Here, car 5 and trailer 46 pass over a farm crossing at Ballellin. (E. Gray)

For most of its route the coastal tramway follows the contours of the land, but at Ballagorry, north of Glen Mona, a deep cutting was necessary. This is spanned by the line's only overbridge. Winter saloon 21, then painted in one of the 'historic' liveries applied in 1979, heads south for Douglas. (E. Gray)

At Cornaa, where there is a small shelter by the northbound track, a sharp curve coincides with a change of grade. Car 1 runs over the minor road crossing on its way from Ramsey to Douglas. (E. Gray)

Between Ballajora and Dreemskerry a siding and headshunt (now lifted) served a quarry which once supplied ballast for the tramway. Still in situ in the quarry, but hidden by dense undergrowth, are two lines of light track, one dual gauge, which led to a primitive tipping gantry above the siding. Winter saloon 19 and trailer 45 pass the quarry in 1981. (E. Gray)

Ramsey Bay and the pier come into view at Belle Vue halt. An alternative scheme for the approach to Ramsey would have taken the course of the line to a lower level. A new promenade was planned at Port-e-Vullen, where unfinished work may still be seen, and the line would have entered Ramsey along the shore line, terminating by the pier. (Roy Brook)

In the event, the original plan to cross Ballure Glen further inland was adopted. From the opening of the Ramsey service on 2 August 1898, pending the completion of the viaduct, the terminus lay near the present Ballure Gardens, where a small depot to house six cars was constructed. A winter saloon and goods van cross southwards over the viaduct.

From Ballure, the extension to the present Ramsey terminus passes over the main road and a short section of private right of way, to a length of reserved track at the side of Walpole Drive. Until 1995 this was laid with grooved tram rail, the only example on the system, a relic of the town's never-fulfilled intention to surface the road. Car 20 with trailer 42 passes southwards along Walpole Drive in 1985. (E. Gray)

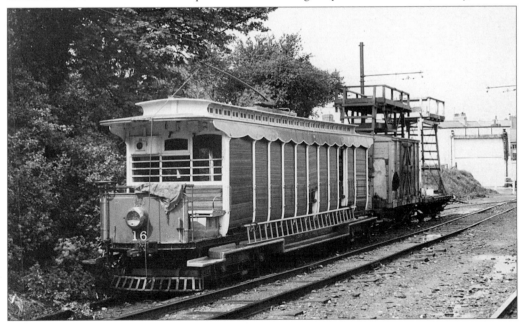

Nearing the end of the line, and on the opposite side of the tracks from the depot building, is the short siding of the former cattle dock, now occasionally used as a convenient stabling point for spare vehicles. Car 16, with its shutters closed and trolley pole tied down, together with two tower wagons, had been left overnight by the poles and wires gang in May 1985. (E. Gray)

Passengers alighting at Ramsey often pause to observe the shunting operations. The power car leaves its trailer to draw forward, then reverses on the cross-over, while the trailer is shunted to the other end by gravity. Car 19, which had also brought goods van 4, carries out this manoeuvre as car 5 waits on the departure line in June 1965. To the right is the wall of the now-demolished Plaza Cinema. (E. Gray)

Car 21 reverses at Ramsey, pre-1910. The service to the present Ramsey terminus at Parsonage Road began on 24 July 1899, the complete line being 17¾ miles long, double-track throughout, with a journey time of 1 hour 15 minutes. Somehow, and sometimes against the odds, the Ramsey section has survived winter closures, and even complete closure to reach its centenary.

THE SNAEFELL MOUNTAIN RAILWAY

Having opened the coastal route to Laxey in 1894, the Isle of Man Tramways & Electric Power Company turned its attention to the construction of a 5-mile line to the summit of Snaefell, 2,036 ft above sea level. A gauge of 3 ft 6 in was chosen, the extra width accommodating a centrally placed Fell patent rail, which could be gripped by a calliper brake when cars were descending steep grades. During the construction of the line, the steam locomotive Caledonia was hired from the Manx Northern Railway to transport materials. The line was completed in time for services to begin in August 1895. Six tramcars (originally unglazed, except for the end platforms) were supplied by G.F. Milnes, with electrical equipment by Mather & Platt once again, together with a sprung version of the Hopkinson bow collector. A hotel was built at the upper terminus. The Snaefell line is the only electrically operated mountain railway in Britain, and the only one to retain the Fell braking equipment. The car trucks have additional brakes, applied by the standard hand-wheel, and rheostatic braking is also employed. The Snaefell cars are the only vehicles that can reach the summit, from where, on clear days, visitors can see England, Ireland, Scotland and Wales.

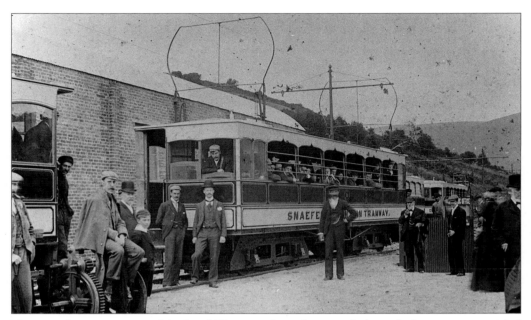

The original Laxey terminus of the Snaefell line was alongside its car shed, to which point passengers had to climb via a flight of steps from the road below. This picture, taken on the opening day, 21 August 1895, includes Dr Edward Hopkinson (sitting on winch, left), adaptor of his brother's bow collector, and George Noble Fell, son of the patentee, with his foot on the rail in front of the car.

At the terminal points, and on certain intermediate lengths, the track was level and therefore not equipped with the Fell braking rail. Right-hand running was adopted for the 1 in 12 ascent. Car 6 stands a little way short of the original Laxey terminus and car shed.

The track bed of the first part of the Snaefell line is cut into the hillside on the southern slopes of the Laxey valley. A substantial stone retaining wall, to which buttresses were added in 1906, was required at Lhergy Veg. Car 4 is ascending on the right-hand track. The Fell rail protrudes above the level of the outer rails. (David Bailey collection)

At the point where the tramway crosses the mountain road between Douglas and Laxey, there was formerly the Bungalow Hotel. The hotel was built on the far side of the road, on the southern side of the line, and though most of the building was demolished in 1958, there still exists a short siding (right). The Bungalow is the only intermediate stopping point en route to the summit.

From the Bungalow station, the Manx Electric Railway offered charabanc tours to its hotel and tea gardens at Tholt-y-Will in Sulby Glen. Two Argus 16-seat vehicles (MN 67 and 68) were used between 1907 and 1914. The service ceased during the war years but resumed in 1920 with new coaches, before being interrupted again by the Second World War.

Resuming the climb from the Bungalow, the tramway winds round the side of Snaefell in a spiral. The high ground is to the right as the car ascends this upper section, and eventually the Laxey valley comes into view again on the left. The gradient levels off as car 5 nears the summit in this 1905 postcard. Note that only the right-hand, descending, track is equipped with Fell rail at this point. (Valentine)

51966 Hotel Summit of Snaefell Mountain, I.O.M. J.V.

The Snaefell Mountain Railway settled into a steady and profitable seasonal routine, commencing services in time for the Whitsuntide holidays and running through until the end of September. The fine turreted and castellated hotel at the upper terminus was built in 1906, and replaced an earlier structure sited nearby. Car 5 stands in wait. (Valentine)

Car 3 on the terminal stub outside the hotel, with the line's open wagon, apparently loaded with coal, at the extremity of the track (left). This small wagon was supplied by the firm of Hurst Nelson, Motherwell, in 1895, and was used to carry supplies to the hotel. The building later lost some of its castellated ornamentation, and was damaged by fire in 1982. It reopened in 1984, and was refurbished in 1995. (David Bailey collection)

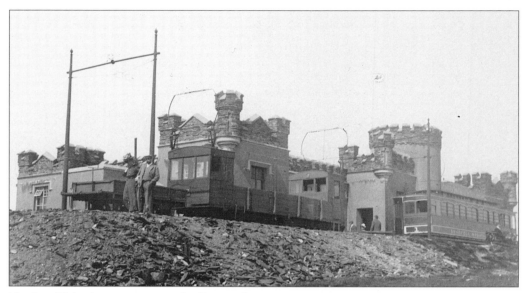

The Snaefell line's strangest item of rolling stock was a 6-ton capacity unpowered open freight car with twin cabs, unofficially dubbed no. 7 *Maria*. When in use, it borrowed trucks and electrical equipment from a passenger car, usually no. 5. Its principal duty was out of season, carrying coal stocks to the power station sited mid-way up the line. On this occasion, in about 1908, it has propelled the wagon to the extremity of the track at the summit. (Manx National Heritage)

At the convergence of the upward and downward tracks at the summit, there is an unusual single-bladed point, the sole survivor of several similar items once in use on the line. The point is normally sprung open to receive cars arriving on the upward track, but is held over by the knee-high lever (right) when cars are departing. (David Bailey collection)

At the lower end of the mountain line, the extension of 1898 into the present terminal area at Laxey created a convenient interchange for Manx Electric and Snaefell passengers. In this 1965 view, MER 19 with trailer and goods van is arriving from Douglas, while Snaefell cars 5 and 6 wait on their terminal stubs. Snaefell 5 sits on the dual-gauge siding, linked to the MER tracks by the cross-over emerging from beneath its bogies. (E. Gray)

Snaefell departures from Laxey are usually half-hourly from 10.30 a.m., according to demand, the journey to the summit taking 30 minutes. The last car normally leaves the summit at 4.30 p.m. The large roofboards were removed from the cars after the 1970 fire which destroyed car 5. It was feared that rocking in high winds might have caused fraying of electric cables. (E. Gray)

In Laxey station the two Snaefell terminal stubs join to become single track for the exit and and road crossing, then divide to commence the climb. Departures are controlled by the stationmaster, who checks that the single-line section is clear. Although right-hand running is the rule, cars going out of service to the depot use the left-hand track. Tracks to the right are the MER lines to Ramsey. (E. Gray)

The Snaefell car shed, built at the side of the 1895 terminus, could accommodate only the six passenger cars, three on each track. Other rolling stock had to remain outside. Car 1, alongside the shed, is on the site of the original station, from where one track was lifted to leave only a single siding. Car 2 is just visible inside the shed. The photograph dates from June 1972. (E. Gray)

In the opposite direction is the approach road to the shed, originally part of the running line. The car in the distance is near the spot where the depot track joins the main line. Space in the shed was restricted, so major maintenance tasks were carried out at the MER workshops. Cars for overhaul were towed from Laxey to Derby Castle on 3 ft gauge accommodation bogies, fitted on the dual gauge siding. (Roy Brook)

In 1970 car 5 caught fire at the summit. The flames, fanned by a high wind, destroyed the body, but the trucks and underframe were salvaged to form the basis for a replica vehicle, constructed by H.D. Kinnin of Ramsey. The new car 5, seen descending past the depot siding, does not have the clerestory roof of the original, and was fitted with bus-type aluminium window frames. (E. Gray)

The open wagon (or the tower wagon when in use) is propelled up the mountain, the braked power car remaining always at the lower end in case of a runaway. Car 2 pushes the wagon on the upward track. The facing points for the depot approach are to the right. In 1977 the six cars were re-equipped with more modern (1956–7) motors, controllers, and roof-mounted resistances, all obtained from redundant vehicles in Aachen. (E. Gray)

The roof-mounted resistances are apparent in this view of car 4 climbing the upper slopes of the mountain. The ruling gradient is 1 in 12. The driver and brakesman have rheostatic braking at their disposal, in addition to the hand brake and the Fell brake. The outdated Hopkinson bow collectors have performed reasonably well in maintaining contact with the overhead power line. (E. Gray)

A new depot for the Snaefell cars opened in 1995. On the same site as the 1895 shed, the new building covers three tracks instead of two, and incorporates workshop facilities. Access to the depot line is from the downward track, where a 'sector plate' (since replaced with a conventional point) once moved both track and Fell rail to permit access. Now the Fell rail is interrupted at the point. (E. Gray)

One of the surprise projects for the celebration of the Snaefell centenary was the restoration and use of the 3 ft gauge steam locomotive *Caledonia* on the upper portion of the mountain line. To work with the engine, trailer 57 from the electric line was fitted with Fell braking gear, and moved by low-loader from Derby Castle in May 1995. (E. Gray)

To run the 3 ft gauge vehicles on the mountain tramway, a third line was laid from the Bungalow to the summit. (A similar extra rail was laid in 1895 at the time of the engine's use in the construction work.) *Caledonia*, last steamed in 1968, was first tested after restoration in December 1994. For use on the mountain line, Fell brake callipers were fitted beneath the front buffer beam. (E. Gray)

A special siding to accommodate engine and carriage was laid at the Bungalow. Braking trials saw *Caledonia* and trailer 57 coupled to Snaefell car 2, which was in attendance to act as an emergency brake if required. The third rail was laid only on the right-hand track, which the locomotive used for both upward and downward journeys. The photograph dates from 7 May 1995. (E. Gray)

Caledonia undertook her first passenger-carrying run on Snaefell during the launch of the International Railway Festival at Easter 1995, returning for a second spell of duty in August. The trips, from the Bungalow to the summit, proved very popular. The locomotive propelled the carriage upwards with much huffing and puffing but the descent on the return was less spectacular. (E. Gray)

The centenary of the Snaefell Mountain Railway occurred on 21 August 1995. During this busy season the cars carried special commemorative headboards, designed by M.A. McCormack at Derby Castle workshops. On the afternoon of the centenary day, all six cars were assembled at the summit, before descending simultaneously, three on each track. (E. Gray)

After 1924, when the Snaefell generating station ceased to supply current, the open freight car no. 7, *Maria*, was used only for engineering work. It appears to have fallen out of use altogether by the mid-1950s, and when photographed in 1962 the semi-derelict body was sitting on old sleepers at the side of the depot, behind the tower wagon and the open truck. (E. Gray)

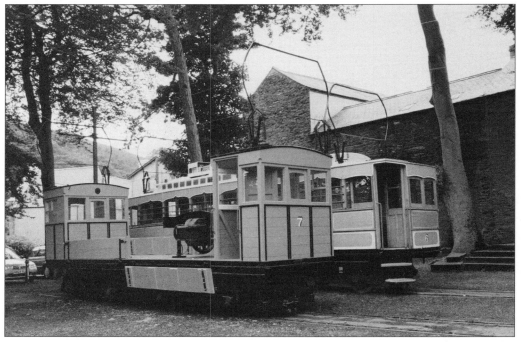

A project that was not quite completed in time for the centenary was the construction of a replica no. 7, *Maria*, here on show in 1997 on the dual-gauge siding alongside car 6 at Laxey. Little of the original *Maria* was in sufficiently good condition to be re-used, but Milnes plate frame trucks and original Mather & Platt motors (fortunately saved from the re-equipping of the 1970s) are fitted. (E. Gray)

THE GROUDLE GLEN RAILWAY

Groudle Glen was leased by R.M. Broadbent in 1893 for development as a tourist attraction. A hotel was built at the entrance, close to the proposed terminus of the new electric tramway from Douglas. Broadbent constructed footpaths and bridges, and planted trees to create an attractive environment, and the glen incorporated such delights as a water wheel, a dance floor and fairground. At the seaward end of the estate, a rocky inlet was enclosed to create a small zoo, into which sea lions and polar bears were introduced. Two cafés were built, one at the zoo and the other on the headland. In 1895, in order to carry passengers to the zoo and cafés, Broadbent began the construction of a 2 ft gauge railway, ¾ mile long, billed as 'the smallest railway in the world'. The track bed was cut into a ledge on the hillside. A single steam locomotive and three carriages were obtained for the start of public services in May 1896. Since then, the line has undergone several changes of fortune, including four periods of closure, but in 1982 the Isle of Man Steam Railway Supporters' Association gained authority to restore the line, and in its care the little railway has prospered and is now safely past its centenary.

Groudle Glen's original locomotive, a 2–4–0 named *Sea Lion*, was supplied in 1896 by the Stafford firm of W.G. Bagnall. The little railway enjoyed immediate success, so much so that the three original coaches proved insufficient to meet demand, and a fourth carriage was ordered.

In 1905, because of the growing popularity of the glen, a second locomotive was obtained from Bagnall's. Four additional coaches were acquired at the same time, so that two trains were available to carry visitors through the glen. The second locomotive, named *Polar Bear*, was similar to the first, the main difference being in the shape of the cab spectacles. (Ranscombe postcard)

The locomotive names were painted on the side tanks, and appeared in a variety of styles over the years. *Polar Bear* is pictured standing at the inland terminus at Lhen Coan (Lovely Glen). A new shed was erected here for the arrival of the second train. To enable the two trains to run simultaneously in busy periods, a passing loop was installed in the single track near the present Lime Kiln Halt.

The railway settled down to steady seasonal operation, but closed during the First World War when visitor traffic ceased. In 1921, because of the post-war rise in coal prices, and the need for overhaul of the steam engines, two battery-electric locomotives were obtained, but these lasted only some six years in service. In 1927 the steam engines were in service again.

The railway suffered its second wartime period of closure after the 1939 season. In the post-war years the glen passed through several changes of ownership. The locomotive *Sea Lion* was unusable, and a section of the track bed was unsafe. Trains operated over a truncated line between 1950 and 1958, but closed again in 1959–60. *Polar Bear* ran in 1961–2 bearing a 'fairground' livery.

After the 1962 season the line closed again, this time, apparently, for good. Both locomotives were in a sorry condition. In 1967 *Polar Bear* was acquired and removed to the Brockham Museum in Surrey, and in 1968 *Sea Lion* was rescued and taken to John Walton's Steam Centre at Kirk Michael, where it remained in derelict condition alongside a traction engine. (E. Gray)

When the line reopened in 1950, and until its closure in 1962, trains terminated on a re-sited headland loop because of worries about the instability of the track bed further on. Buildings were demolished, and most of the track lifted after sale of the glen in 1967, but some overgrown track remaining beyond the headland was being used in 1983 to park some preservationists' wagons. (E. Gray)

The original run-round terminal loop at Sea Lion Rocks had not been used since 1939, but the track, with check rails, remained embedded in the ground. The stone stop-block (upper centre) was built in 1905 to prevent trains over-running the loop, for immediately beyond is a sheer drop into the cove. (E. Gray)

The movement to re-open the Groudle Glen Railway gained momentum in 1982, when the Steam Railway Supporters' Association, its offers of help on the main railway rejected, turned its attention to Groudle. Volunteers began the task of reviving the line, which was achieved in part by 1983, with a line to the headland by 1985. Viewed from Howstrake, the little train is seen negotiating the hillside. (E. Gray)

The locomotive *Sea Lion* was regained, and apprentices of British Nuclear Fuels at Sellafield undertook its complete restoration. In the meantime, trains were hauled by two 1952 diesel locomotives, *Dolphin* and *Walrus*, obtained from Doddington Park. In 1987 *Sea Lion* returned to the glen to operate on its original line for the first time in nearly forty years. (E. Gray)

For the 'Year of Railways' celebrations in 1993, *Polar Bear*, restored by the Brockham Museum Association, returned to the island for a short season, on loan from the Amberley Chalk Pits Museum. The two original locomotives were thus seen together again. *Polar Bear*, in yellow livery, stands under the replica canopy (right), behind the figure of preservationist Tony Beard. (E. Gray)

Polar Bear climbs through the wooded hillside towards Lime Kiln Halt in September 1993, shortly before its return to the mainland. Three original Groudle 4-wheel coaches accompanied the engine from Amberley, offering a different ride from the line's own bogie stock. The two locomotives operated a number of double-headed workings during the visit. (E. Gray)

Precedents having been established for the exchange of locomotives, the line's centenary year saw two popular visitors from the Leighton Buzzard Narrow Gauge Railway at work on the Groudle line. The vertical-boilered engine *Chaloner*, built by De Winton of Caernarvon in 1877, leads a train away from Sea Lion Rocks in August 1996. (E. Gray)

Sea Lion and the second 1996 visitor *Rishra*, built by Baguley in 1921 for a pumping station in Calcutta, double-head a train negotiating the headland curve. Traces of the old track formation can be discerned to the left of the train. The whole length of the original line from Lhen Coan to Sea Lion Rocks, approximately ¾ mile long, was fully restored by 1992, some fifty-three years after the last section had been abandoned because of fears that a retaining wall supporting the track bed might collapse. Major earthworks were undertaken on this length to move the track further inland and re-align it away from the cliff edge. The Groudle Glen Railway Company Limited, a wholly owned subsidiary of the Supporters' Association, now operates the railway. Services are staffed by volunteers, and trains run during the season on Sundays, Bank Holidays, and occasional summer evenings. (E. Gray)

Rishra at Sea Lion Rocks terminal loop. Volunteers observed that this locomotive had very similar driving characteristics to *Sea Lion*. The two were the only surviving locomotives to carry the 'improved Baguley valve gear' and both made the same sound when running in service. The pairing of the two engines was most successful. (E. Gray)

The vertical-boilered, ancient-looking *Chaloner* spent most of its working life in the slate quarries of North Wales before being purchased in the early 1960s for preservation. Workers praised its performance on the Groudle line, where it was well able to haul heavy trains unassisted. (E. Gray)

The mainstay of the regular services is, of course, the locomotive *Sea Lion*, subject of a permanent loan agreement for as long as the railway continues to operate. It is maintained in splendid condition. The locomotive is seen here at the head of a train emerging from the wooded section of the line into the sunlight at Lime Kiln Halt on its way to Sea Lion Rocks. (E. Gray)

Sea Lion arrives, blowing off excess steam, at the terminus of the line. Below the maker's plate on the cab side is a second plaque to record the restoration by British Nuclear Fuels. To reciprocate the loans of mainland locomotives, in May 1997 *Sea Lion* visited the Festiniog Railway, a Bagnall loco gathering in Staffordshire, and the Leighton Buzzard Railway. (E. Gray)

DOUGLAS SOUTHERN ELECTRIC TRAMWAY

The Douglas Southern Electric Tramway originated from a concession to construct a line along the route of the Douglas Head Marine Drive. The drive, cut into a ledge on the cliff face, was completed in 1893, but construction of the tramway did not begin until later. The 3½ mile line, single with passing loops, was laid on the landward side of the road, and was the only standard gauge (4 ft 8½ in) track on the island. Opened in July 1896, it ran southwards from Douglas Head, via the right-hand arch of the 1891 toll gates, to Port Soderick. At each end of the route, inclined railways carried passengers to or from the termini. The tramway operated only seasonally, the Marine Drive Company originally receiving one penny for every passenger carried, plus a percentage of the gross receipts. In 1926, on the expiry of the concession, the two companies amalgamated under the title Douglas Head Marine Drive Ltd. Operation had ceased during the First World War, but resumed in 1919. From the end of the 1939 season, and throughout the Second World War, the tramway remained closed but intact. After the war, the company sold its assets to the Isle of Man Highways Board, and the tramway never re-opened. Of the 16 tramcars still resting in the depot as late as 1951, car 1 was rescued and is now an exhibit at the National Tramway Museum in Derbyshire. The depot and the remaining cars were scrapped. On the island today, only the ornamental arch remains.

The Douglas Southern Electric tramway began services with six motor cars (1–6) and six trailers (7–12). Car 3 is seen here at the Douglas Head terminus on the occasion of a directors' special working at the ceremonial opening of the line on 16 July 1896. The return fare to Port Soderick was one shilling. (Manx National Heritage)

Car 4 stands on Douglas Head, with the bay and harbour in the background. The inclined railway of 1900, connecting the tram terminus with the harbour, lay to the right of the picture. On the high ground of the Head (left) was a complex of buildings offering assorted entertainments, including a *camera obscura*, waxworks, side-shows and an observation tower.

South of the Toll Gate entrance arch to the Marine Drive, a long loop on the seaward side of the line was used to park spare car sets or trailers, ready for immediate use if required. As the car depot was sited on a distant and isolated spot further along the line, at one time it was also the practice to leave a motor car on this loop overnight for use by early morning staff. Operation was usually from 10.00 a.m. to 7.30 p.m.

This mid-1930s view of car 6 at the Douglas Head loop clearly shows the location of the terminus in relation to the harbour below. On all the motor cars, the trolley-mast was mounted on the landward side of the top deck, and, as the roadway was always on the seaward side of the track, both staircases faced the opposite side. The canvas blinds were a later addition. (C. Carter)

Car 4 at the Douglas Head terminal loop, post-1926. As it was such a short line, the cars had no real need of destination indicators, but PORT SODERICK was displayed on both ends, with the owning company's title along the side. The car bodies were built by the Brush Company, and mounted on 'Lord Baltimore' trucks, with Westinghouse electrical gear on cars 1–6. (David Bailey collection)

At a nominal speed of 8 miles per hour, a 10-minute frequency was advertised, with 30 minutes allowed for the journey. In fact, the frequency was adjusted according to demand, and the particular passing loops to be used depended upon the number of cars in service. The pattern of operation was indicated to crews by the numbered disc hung over the dash plate. Corresponding numbers were painted on poles at the appropriate passing places. (The late B.Y. Williams)

Impressive engineering features along the line included the bridges at Pigeon Stream (where the line's power station was sited), Wallberry Gap and Horse Leap chasm. This official Douglas Southern Electric postcard of about 1906 is titled 'Approach to Wallberry Bridge,' and shows a single car, dwarfed by the cliffside, about to cross the twin-span viaduct.

This is another official postcard showing a car on the sharp curve at The Whing, and is a good illustration of the location of the roadside track and the landward poles and bracket arms supporting the overhead wires.

Car 6 begins the crossing of Wallberry viaduct on its way to Port Soderick in 1934. Single cars operating without trailers were better able to maintain speed and keep to schedule. The livery of the cars was red and cream, with red panels lined-out in gold. (The late B.Y. Williams)

Port Soderick developed as a favourite leisure centre for visitors to the island. The terminus of the Douglas Southern tramway was on the high cliff (top left). The two coaches of the inclined railway, which conveyed passengers to the beach, may be seen in mid-journey. The course of the line back to Douglas was along the cliffs top right, but holiday-makers could choose to return by steam train or boat.

The trailer cars were identical to the motor cars, except for the lack of electrical equipment. In fact, cars 7 and 8, originally trailers, were converted to power cars in 1897–8 by the provision of General Electric motors and controllers. At the same time an order was placed with the Brush Company for the supply of four additional trailers, numbered 13–16, to the same design, bringing the fleet total to 8 motor cars and 8 trailers. (W.A. Camwell/NTM)

The car shed was constructed in a lonely and isolated spot mid-way along the line at Little Ness. At a level a little lower than the driveway, it was possibly the only piece of flat land available. The timber and corrugated iron building had to be lengthened in 1897 in order to house four cars on each of the four tracks. Here, car 6 stands outside, its canvas blinds lowered, in the 1930s. (W.A. Camwell/NTM)

Inside the car shed, two of the four tracks had inspection pits for part of their length. Car 4 (also displaying disc 4) sits on the seaward track during the long sleep of 1939–51. On Friday 15 September 1939 a three-car service had operated on the last day of the season, after which the depot had been closed for the winter and the electricity supply turned off.

In 1951, largely owing to the efforts of F.K. Pearson, car 1 was extracted from the shed and subsequently restored for display, first at Clapham, and now at Crich, Derbyshire. Outside the shed, someone had hung the symbolic 'LC' disc, which was used to indicate to crews the LAST CAR of the day. The shed and the remaining fifteen cars were scrapped on site.

THE 1990S

The Manx Electric Railway, the Snaefell Mountain Railway, and the Groudle Glen Railway all celebrated their centenaries in the 1990s, and the steam railway approached its 125th year. The depressing period of asset-stripping and closures appeared to have passed, and, with a new chief executive in charge, the vintage transport systems (since 1986 grouped under the Department of Tourism and Transport) were at last appreciated for their real value. The centenary of the Manx Electric line to Groudle was chosen to be the 'Isle of Man Year of Railways 1993,' and special events were organised by co-ordinator Alan Corlett. Designed to draw enthusiasts to the island and to introduce newcomers to the delights of the Victorian vehicles, the celebrations were highly successful. It is estimated that the events attracted some 18,000 extra visitors, and brought a much-needed boost to the tourist industry. So successful were these events that the formula, with new variations each time, was repeated to mark other anniversaries. With the opening of the Ramsey visitor centre, the improvements to workshops and depots, and projected refurbishments to the Port Erin Museum, it became clear that the island authorities were ready to invest more capital in their transport treasures. The year 1998 marks the centenary of the tramway extension to Ramsey and the 125th year of the steam railway.

A steam locomotive working on an electric tramway is an unusual sight guaranteed to excite transport enthusiasts. In the construction of the tramway between Laxey and Ramsey in 1898, steam locomotives had been hired to haul works trains. To commemorate this event no. 4, *Loch*, was transferred to haul passenger carriages on the tramway during the 1993 celebrations. (E. Gray)

The locomotive was stabled in Laxey tram shed overnight, and on scheduled demonstration runs, hauled trailers 57 and 58 from a special siding as far as Dhoon Quarry. The landward, northbound track was used in both directions, so service cars to Ramsey had to work 'wrong-line' until a suitable cross-over was reached. Car 7 runs parallel as *Loch* begins the climb from Laxey. (E. Gray)

Test runs had been made in advance to check that the steam loco could cope with the gradients and curves on the tramway and consequently the number of carriages hauled was limited to two. Here, *Loch* makes a great deal of black smoke as she works hard, pounding up the slope near Minorca on the long climb to the summit in September 1993. (E. Gray)

At the summit of the tramway near Ballaragh, the locomotive's hard work was over, and *Loch* could drift with minimum effort round the curve at Dhoon Glen on the way to Dhoon Quarry. Before the return journey, the engine's water tanks were replenished from a tank at the quarry which had been sited alongside a siding specially laid in for the event. (E. Gray)

At Dhoon Quarry the locomotive ran round its trailers and returned to Laxey bunker first on the landward track. Driver John Elkin has steam to spare as he coaxes *Loch* on the approach to the summit in June 1993. The number of passengers allowed on these popular trips was strictly limited, but reservations could be made via a system of advance booking. (E. Gray)

In addition to the unusual sight of a steam locomotive operating on an electric tramway, photographers were also intrigued by the opportunities offered in capturing a tramcar on 'wrong-line' workings. Ramsey-bound car 20 climbs wrong-line past Minorca during steam runs on the adjoining track. (E. Gray)

The decade started badly for the electric tramway when, on the night of 30 September/1 October 1990, the body of car 22 was destroyed by fire in the lower shed at Derby Castle. A replica body was constructed by contractors McArd of Port Erin, and equipped and mounted on the frames and trucks of the original 22 by MER staff. The new 22 is seen here at Dhoon Glen in July 1994. (E. Gray)

The crossbench cars without air brake equipment have seen little use since the 1970s. After the attempted sale of four of them in 1978, most have remained in store, some being cannibalised to keep others in service. Car 18 has been the only serviceable hand-braked car available, and has proved popular on journeys between Douglas and Laxey during enthusiasts' weeks. (E. Gray)

The fourth track in Laxey shed was home to the remains of the redundant steeple cab locomotive 23 for many years. Built at Derby Castle in 1900 for the haulage of stone traffic, it was driven on trucks and equipment borrowed from a passenger car. Rebuilt in 1925 after an earlier accident, it lay idle after 1944. In 1965 the body was sitting on piles of old sleepers. (E. Gray)

Locomotive 23 was possibly the most unusual item of rolling stock owned by the electric railway. In its 1925 rebuilding, the original cab was rescued and mounted between two wagon bodies. Restored as a result of efforts by the Isle of Man Railway Society, in 1992 it was named *Dr R. Preston Hendry* in memory of the founder and chairman of the society. (E. Gray)

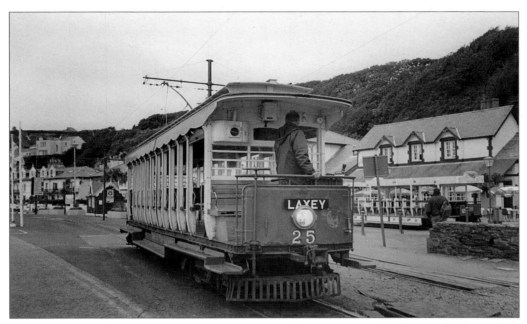

Manx Electric tramcars do not carry destination display fittings. Some early photographs show saloon vehicles carrying small boards in clips below the centre windows, reading LAXEY or RAMSEY, but nowadays these are not required. Here, on 9 September 1993, car 25 is pictured at Derby Castle terminus with a destination board tucked in behind the rim of the dashplate lamp. (E. Gray)

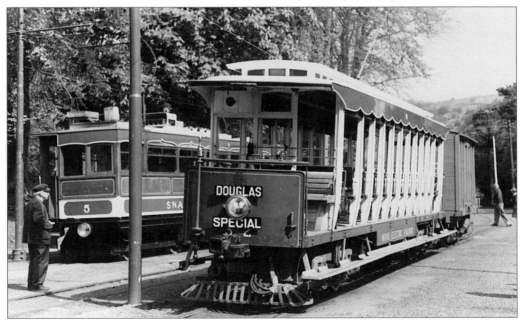

At Laxey on 4 May 1995, the headlamp rim of car 32 was holding the two plates of a Douglas Special working during an enthusiasts' week. The car was towing one of the goods vans. Snaefell 5, waiting for mountain line passengers, was damaged by fire in 1970, and has a replica body boasting a low-slung headlamp. (E. Gray)

Popular features of the enthusiasts' weeks have been 'Motorman Lessons', offering unique and pleasurable opportunities to drive a vintage tramcar – under supervision, and without passengers, of course! Instructor Mike Goodwyn stands on the footboard as the writer's wife Kathleen tries her hand on car 16 between Laxey and Douglas. (E. Gray)

In 1992 a 200hp Schoema 4-wheel diesel locomotive, built new in 1958, was purchased second-hand from Germany to be used principally for works trains and stand-by duties on the steam railway. Seen outside the workshops, it was allocated the number 17 and named *Viking* at a ceremony in 1993. (E. Gray)

In the 1994 season Manx Electric car 20 ran with a headboard commemorating the centenary of the Lonan Parish Commission. The car is seen at the end of the track at Derby Castle, ready to depart on the journey to Ramsey. The rustic booking office (right) dates from 1897 and lies between the electric and horse-tram tracks. (E. Gray)

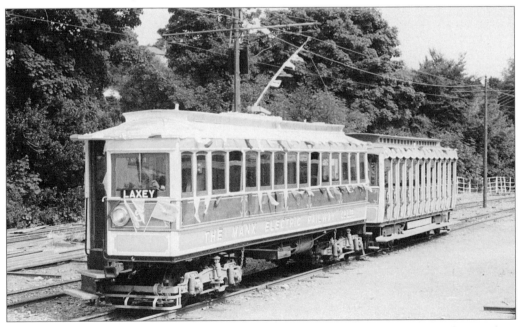

The centenary of the electric tramway extension to Laxey was commemorated on 28 July 1994 by a special run of car 5 and trailer, adorned with bunting for the occasion, and bearing a destination plate below the driver's windscreen. The location is the approach to the Glen Roy viaduct, the site of the second (1896–7) Laxey terminus after Rencell Road had been bridged. (E. Gray)

During the special events organised in July 1994, in order to entertain the photographers and, no doubt, to confuse future historians, two cars destroyed in the 1930 depot fire at Laxey were 're-created' by temporarily renumbering cars 6 and 2 as '8' and '3'. On their inaugural outing, they ran in parallel to Groudle, and are seen on their return journey approaching Howstrake. (E. Gray)

Still masquerading as car 3, car 2 was photographed later the same day towing trailer 13 on the curve near the road crossing at Ballabeg. On this busy road, lights to warn motorists of the approach of a tramcar are activated by the passage of the tram wheels over contacts in the track. Driver Bob Clarke is muffled against the weather, but the trailer passengers look summery. (E. Gray)

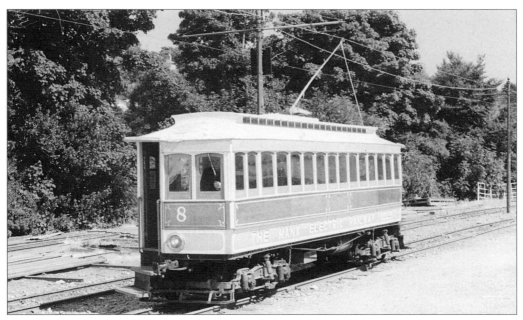

Similarly, car 6 entered service in disguise as number 8 on the Laxey centenary day, and is seen approaching Laxey at the sub-station site at Rencell Road. Observers of car body details were able to recognise car 6 by the twin windows of the driving platform, reinstated in 1992–3. (E. Gray)

Among the events held in July 1994 on both the steam railway and the electric tramway were demonstrations by Capt. Stephen Carter of a recently restored vertical-boilered steam-powered crane, IMR no. 3. It was here being towed to Laxey by crossbench car 33, with the permanent way department's flat wagon deployed in between to protect the jib. (E. Gray)

Crossbench paddlebox 27 has been employed for some years as the works car for the poles and wires gang, and is often seen loaded with assorted tools and towing a tower wagon. In 1993–4, because it is used on much winter maintenance work, it was fitted with a partial vestibule at each end to protect the driver from the worst of the weather. (E. Gray)

Car 27 had brought trailer 61 from Derby Castle for winter storage at Laxey when this photograph was taken in 1994. The towing car had uncoupled and reversed on to the depot headshunt as the trailer rolled past by gravity; car 27 is about to reverse again, collect the trailer, and propel it into the depot. The distorted appearance of 27's nearside is due to the vestibule fitment. (E. Gray)

At Derby Castle depot in July 1994 this line-up illustrates variations in the styles of painting crossbench cars. Car 18 has a black frame, with roof, bargeboards, and side pillars all in white; 33 has a red frame and bargeboards, varnished pillars and matching brown trucks; 26 has white pillars and roof with red bargeboards. (E. Gray)

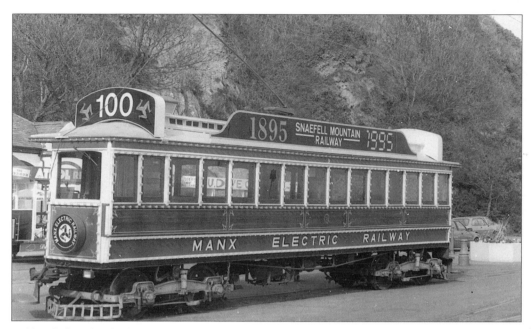

Unlike Blackpool and other cities, it was a long time before the Isle of Man gained an illuminated tramcar. Tram no. 9 was fitted out to celebrate the tramway centenary in 1993, and with minor modifications was adapted to advertise the 1995 centenary of the Snaefell Mountain Railway. The blaze of light it created proved very popular on evening runs to Groudle. (E. Gray)

A popular feature of the enthusiasts' weeks has been the parallel running of two cars on adjoining tracks. For safety reasons, these unusual workings are scheduled to take place before the start of the day's normal services. The two surviving 1893 vehicles are the oldest tramcars still working on their original line anywhere in the world. These two are pictured at Howstrake in May 1995. (E. Gray)

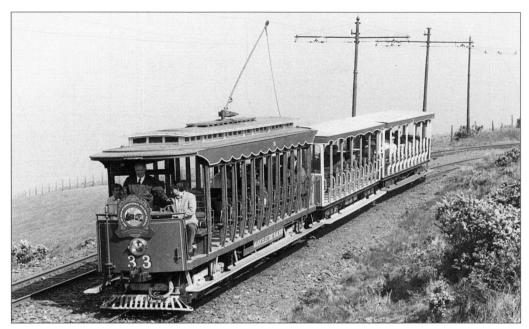

For the benefit of photographers, a departure from usual practice in May 1995 saw a demonstration run of a tram hauling two trailers from Douglas to Ramsey. Driven by the then Engineering Superintendent Maurice Faragher, car 33 (displaying the special headboard of the 'International Festival of Railways') is seen with trailers 37 and 60 at the Ballaragh summit. (E. Gray)

Another much-appreciated innovation during the Snaefell Centenary celebrations in August 1995 was an *Old Hands' Special*, an occasion for former employees to practise their old skills and enjoy a reunion with workmates. Car 22, with its new body, was used as far as Laxey, where the party transferred to a Snaefell car for the ascent to the summit hotel. (E. Gray)

In 1995 another example of temporary renumbering led to the re-appearance of lost car number '4,' unseen since 1930. This was, of course, car 6 again in new guise to please the photographers and enthusiasts. It is seen on the reverse curves approaching Garwick in May 1995. (E. Gray)

In August 1995 car 6 was still operating as car '4'. Rostered for a Douglas–Laxey working, it had run round its trailer and was propelling it past the Mines Tavern towards the siding by the goods shed, a usual lay-by for extra car sets to wait clear of service cars on the main line. (E. Gray)

Another 1995 resurrection of a lost car was no. '24,' in reality car 26, seen here at Baldrine, driven by Mike Goodwyn. Close examination revealed that the new numbers were merely removable plastic stick-ons. (E. Gray)

Car 26 remained in the guise of car '24' for much of the season. Pictured on the morning of 5 May 1995, after working an extra journey to Laxey, it passes through the trees on the Garwick curve, returning to Douglas passenger-less to collect more visitors for Snaefell. (E. Gray)

The year 1995 saw the completion of work on trailer 56 to convert it to a saloon carriage for the conveyance of disabled passengers. The trailer retains its clerestory roof and bulkheads, but now has glazed sides and is equipped with removable seating, folding entrance steps and a wheelchair hoist. It is seen behind car 7 at the Derby Castle terminus in August 1995. (E. Gray)

In 1994 car 25 was withdrawn from passenger service and subsequently acted as the Ramsey-based works car. Here, on 5 May 1995, it is in use by the track repair team on the outskirts of Ramsey as car 20 passes by. Car 20 was being driven by transport Chief Executive Robert Smith, keeping in practice, with the regular motorman at his side. (E. Gray)

The Manx Northern Railway's 1885 locomotive *Caledonia*, unused since the 1960s and long-time exhibit in the Port Erin Museum, was the subject of an intensive restoration programme in 1993–4 in preparation for the centenary of the Snaefell tramway, in whose construction she had been used. The brass numerals receive a final polish at Douglas. (E. Gray)

Caledonia re-appeared in her original 'Metropolitan Red' livery, with gold leaf lettering and ornamental scrollwork. After tests, the inaugural run on the steam railway took place at Easter 1995. The engine is seen here at the head of a four-coach Port Erin train as it slows to collect a mother and baby at the Ballabeg request halt. (E. Gray)

Caledonia's return to service included a number of special duties during the spring and summer celebrations. On 3 May 1995 the engine hauled a works train of flat wagons loaded with sleepers, and is seen in the spring sunshine passing through the woods at Crogga en route for Ballasalla. (E. Gray)

The locomotive was also rostered to work several regular service trains to Port Erin, and is here seen on the cliff tops at Keristal on the approach to Port Soderick on 24 July 1995. Although the original Manx Northern number was painted on the tank sides, *Caledonia* retained her IMR no. 15 chimney with the brass numerals. (E. Gray)

For the benefit of railway enthusiasts in general and photographers in particular, some double-headed runs were arranged during the season. *Caledonia* is here making dense black smoke as she starts away from Castletown, piloting no. 10 *G.H. Wood* on the pumphouse curve. (E. Gray)

Caledonia undertook spells of duty on both the electric tramway and the upper portion of the Snaefell line in 1995. On the Manx Electric Railway *Caledonia*, seen here climbing over the Minorca viaduct, ran as *Loch* had done in 1993, between Laxey and Dhoon Quarry, but hauled only trailer 58, as 57 remained at the Bungalow siding for use on the Snaefell line. (E. Gray)

Locomotive no. 6, *Peveril*, which in the late 1970s had been offered to the National Railway Museum in York, did not, in fact, leave the island. The engine was thus available for a cosmetic restoration exercise carried out by members of the Isle of Man Steam Railway Supporters' Association, and proved a popular static exhibit at Douglas. (E. Gray)

In 1995 the sight of *Caledonia* moving about the island on a low-loader became almost commonplace. Having been taken to Snaefell for test runs, the engine returned to the steam railway for modifications, worked on the mountain line in May, then on both the steam and the electric lines, before moving again on 20 August from Laxey for a second spell on Snaefell. (E. Gray)

Replacement of the old upper sheds at Derby Castle tramway depot began in 1997. Many items of rolling stock had to be stored temporarily elsewhere. From the already refurbished lower shed workshops, car 19 emerged after overhaul, resplendent in the livery style of 1899. Behind the car, the unfinished new shed awaited completion of its full track connections. (E. Gray)

After receiving its major rebuild, winter saloon 19 re-entered service in July 1997. Its 1899 cream-and-brown livery was in readiness for the centenary of the completion of the line to Ramsey, and the car's own centenary in 1999. The modernity of the scene at Laxey is betrayed only by the costumes and the plastic waste bin. (E. Gray)

The practice of temporarily re-numbering tramcars during the enthusiasts' weeks in order to 'recreate' vehicles which have been destroyed was given a new twist when paddlebox 26 was re-numbered as 42. This, in fact, was a number which it had once carried. The 24–27 series cars were delivered as trailers in 1898, but were motorised and re-numbered by the new company in 1903. (E. Gray)

Paddlebox 26 appeared disguised as '42' for periods in both 1996 and 1997, but the stickers were then removed. However, on the inside of the Douglas-end bulkhead the number 42 can still be discerned in faded numerals applied a century ago. Car 26 was repainted by volunteers from the Manx Electric Railway Society in 1992. It is shown here at Ballabeg in July 1997. (E. Gray)

Special night photography sessions were organised for transport enthusiasts on both the steam railway and the electric tramway. At Laxey on 24 July 1997 Engineering Superintendent George Lawson had the happy idea of lining up Manx Electric cars 1 and 2 with Snaefell 3. (E. Gray)

It is hoped that the decrepit Laxey Car Shed will be replaced in the not-too-distant future. The depot houses the engineering car, tower wagons, and one or two serviceable cars, but mainly unusable rolling stock. Ratchets 15, 28, 29 and 30 have been stored here for some twenty years, joined since by cars 14 and 17, the latter damaged in the 1992 Derby Castle fire which destroyed car 22. (E. Gray)

Events planned to celebrate the 125th anniversary of the steam railway in 1998 include the return to service of the IMR's oldest locomotive, no. 1, *Sutherland*, of 1873. Extracted from the Port Erin Museum, the engine, seen here in Douglas workshops in July 1997 with the boiler removed from the frames, has been dismantled and work is proceeding to fit a refurbished boiler. (E. Gray)

The railway workshops at Douglas are an industrial archaeologist's delight. The drive belts to the machines were once powered by this stationary steam engine, still in working order, supplied by John Chadwick's Prince's Bridge Ironworks, which, despite the name, were actually in Salford. Some Salford firms, like Mather & Platt, used 'Manchester' in the address because the larger town was better known. Notice the spare bell-mouth brass dome on the rack behind. (E. Gray)

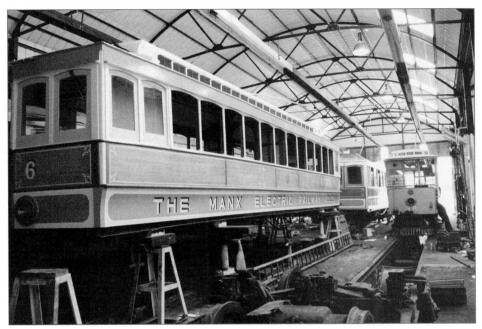

The Derby Castle workshops of the Manx Electric Railway are likewise preparing for the 1998 celebration of the extension of the tramway to Ramsey. In mid-1997 trucks had been removed from under car 6, whose body was undergoing extensive overhaul. Car 32, on the adjoining line, was receiving minor repairs to the air brake system. (E. Gray)

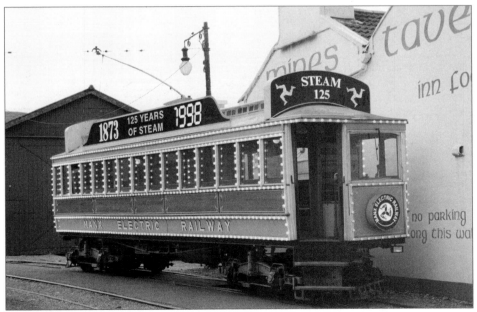

In 1997 illuminated car 9 was advertising forthcoming attractions by drawing attention to the '1873–1998 125 Years Of Steam' celebrations. On its exterior it carries over 1,600 lamp bulbs. With appropriate modification to the wording of the display panels, it has been in use each year since its first appearance for the 1993 tramway centenary. The vehicle reached its own centenary in 1994. (E. Gray)

ACKNOWLEDGEMENTS

This pictorial coverage of the history of Isle of Man transport is very much a secondary work. The writer's late father spoke with great fondness of island holidays at Cunningham's Camp in Douglas, but it was only in the post-war period that the writer himself discovered the delights of the island. Too late to ride the cable cars, or sample the Douglas Head Marine Drive tramway, he nevertheless considers himself fortunate in having seen the complete railway system (though he had to walk the Foxdale line) and in having met some of the legendary characters, such as railway manager A.M. Sheard and St John's stationmaster George Crellin.

The photographs in this book have been compiled from a variety of sources over a considerable period. Illustrations are individually acknowledged where the origin is known, and apologies are offered for any inadvertent omissions. David Bailey of Warrington generously allowed access to his private collection, and the writer is indebted to the following individuals and groups for permission to reproduce photographs: Roy Brook; C. Carter; Robert P. Hendry; Arthur Kirby; Manx National Heritage (Manx Museum); the National Railway Museum (Locomotive & General Photographs); Graham Stacey of R.A.S. Marketing; Eric Sutcliffe (of Weir Pumps Ltd, incorporating Mather & Platt); and Adrian Vaughan. The valued assistance of Miss Wendy Thirkettle of the Manx Museum, Arthur Haynes, and Westbrook Photography is acknowledged with thanks. Alan Palmer of Worsley kindly compiled the map of the island's rail systems.

Detailed histories of the various island transport systems have been consulted for much of the information used in the captions. The original work and researches of the following authors are acknowledged with admiration and gratitude:

J.I.C. Boyd, *The Isle Of Man Railway*, 3 vols, Oakwood Press, 1993–6
A.M. Goodwyn, *Manx Electric*, Platform 5, 1993
A.M. Goodwyn, *Douglas Head Marine Drive Tramway*, MER Society, 1978/93
A.M. Goodwyn, *Snaefell Mountain Railway*, MER Society, 1987
Dr R. Preston Hendry & R. Powell Hendry, *Manx Northern*, Hillside Publishing, 1980
N. Jones, *Isle of Man Railways & Tramways*, Foxline, 1993/4
F.K. Pearson, *Isle Of Man Tramways*, David & Charles, 1970
F.K. Pearson & S. Basnett, *Double Century*, Adam Gordon, 1996
D.M. Smith, *The Groudle Glen Railway*, Plateway Press, 1989

Issues of the MER Society's *Manx Transport Review* and the Railway Supporters' Association *Manx Steam Railway News* have provided detailed information on day-to-day events. Richard Dodge and other island-based enthusiasts have provided much background material. As always, the writer's wife Kathleen has been more than supportive throughout and, since partaking of a 'Motorman Lesson', has become almost as enthusiastic as him in the love of Manx vintage transport.

No expression of thanks would be complete without mention of the warm welcome extended to visitors by members of railway and tramway staff, many of whom, as a result of regular visits, the writer regards almost as old friends. Mike Goodwyn, Darryl Gribbin, George Lawson, John Matthews, and others known by sight, if not by name, have all made significant contributions in their various ways, and their patience and tolerance of an amateur's interest has been appreciated. Mere expressions of thanks seem inadequate for the man who makes it all happen – Alan Corlett. Since his appointment as co-ordinator for the 'Year of Railways' in 1993, Alan Corlett has been ingenious in dreaming up schemes to delight transport enthusiasts. Amazingly, the authorities agree to his plans. During these special events, he is to be seen serving breakfasts, setting out traffic cones, acting as compère, guiding parties round the sheds, lighting the barbecue, etc. – all part of his day's work. Thank you, Alan.

BRITAIN IN OLD PHOTOGRAPHS

To order any of these titles please telephone our distributor, Littlehampton Book Services on 01903 721596
For a catalogue of these and our other titles please ring Regina Schinner on 01453 731114